EFFECTIVE SANCTIONS ON SOUTH AFRICA

EFFECTIVE SANCTIONS ON SOUTH AFRICA

The Cutting Edge of Economic Intervention

Edited by
GEORGE W. SHEPHERD, JR.

*Published under the auspices of the
Consortium on Human Rights Development*

Studies in Human Rights, Number 11

GREENWOOD PRESS
New York • Westport, Connecticut • London

Library of Congress Cataloging-in-Publication Data

Effective sanctions on South Africa : the cutting edge of economic
  intervention / edited by George W. Shepherd, Jr.
    p. cm. — (Studies in human rights, ISSN 0146-3586 ; no. 11)
  "Published under the auspices of the Consortium on Human Rights
Development."
  Includes bibliographical references and index.
  ISBN 0-313-27529-7 (lib. bdg. : alk. paper)
  1. Economic sanctions—South Africa. I. Shepherd, George W., Jr.
II. University of Denver. Consortium on Human Rights Development.
III. Series.
HF1613.4.E34   1991
337.1'68—dc20   90-37840

British Library Cataloguing in Publication Data is available.

A paperback edition of *Effective Sanctions on South Africa* is available from
the Praeger Publishers imprint of Greenwood Publishing Group, Inc.
(ISBN 0-275-93714-3).

Library of Congress Catalog Card Number: 90-37840
ISBN: 0-313-27529-7
ISSN: 0146-3586

First published in 1991

Greenwood Press, 88 Post Road West, Westport, CT 06881
An imprint of Greenwood Publishing Group, Inc.

Printed in the United States of America

The paper used in this book complies with the
Permanent Paper Standard issued by the National
Information Standards Organization (Z39.48-1984).

10 9 8 7 6 5 4 3 2 1

Contents

Introduction: The Role of International Sanctions against South Africa

____George W. Shepherd, Jr.____

There has been a long-standing debate in international circles over the effectiveness of sanctions, and the generally accepted conclusion has been that they are not effective.[1] While there is much evidence that this has been true in the past,[2] the world is rapidly changing. The emerging results in South Africa are different: as the South African weekly *Financial Mail* put it, "Don't Kid Yourself, Effective Sanctions Do Work."[3] What this indicates about the changing nature of the international order and in particular the capacity of the world system to act in response to flagrant violations of human rights is a major issue.[4]

Internationalist and liberal views of the world have tended to favor the use of economic sanctions through multilateral agencies to punish violators of peace and justice.[5] Conservatives and nationalists have viewed military and especially unilateral force as a more appropriate means of preserving their concept of the national sovereign interests.[6] Third World and nonaligned spokespersons have been particularly strong advocates of the use of economic means, through the United Nations and other regional associations, to uphold agreed standards of international conduct.[7] Western political leaders have frequently complained that these measures were "double standards," unfairly applied only to the conduct of major Western powers rather than violations of Third World powers themselves.[8] In general, however, major powers such as the United States and the USSR have been more likely to use unilateral sanctions than accept international law and agencies as the major means of implementing either military or economic sanctions. The superpower has been the last bastion of sovereignty on the matter of sanctions.

Another issue is the effect within South African society of external pressures. White South Africans of all political persuasions—from Pik Botha to Alan Paton and Helen Sussman—as well as scholars like Lawrence Schlemmer and business spokesmen such as Sir Robert Oppenheimer, have viewed sanctions as detrimental to the solution of their problems. A number of White South Africans in exile—for example, Mary Benson, Leslie Rubin, Joe Slovo, and Jennifer Davis—have strongly championed the cause of international sanctions and have contributed extensively to the organized campaigns in Western countries for such actions. They have also supported African liberation movements like the ANC who were the primary advocates of international military bans and economic boycotts.

In the West, the academic controversy over sanctions during the 1970s was the prelude to the political debate that erupted in the 1980s. The result was the U.S. Congressional Comprehensive Anti-Apartheid Act of 1986 and the Commonwealth and European Community actions of 1986–1987.[9] The freeing of Nelson Mandela from prison in South Africa and his visit to the United States and other Western countries in mid-1990 marked the beginning of a new phase in the sanctions debate. Sanctions have demonstrated their effectiveness by freeing political prisoners and ending the state of emergency in South Africa, thus enabling African political groups to function more freely and enter into negotiations. But the question became, Could international sanctions be maintained as an effective instrument for strengthening the position of the Africans in negotiations for a just settlement of outstanding differences between the weaker majority African side and the dominant white minority? Similar opposite positions emerged as in the earlier debate. Africans, Western liberals and socialists, and the Third World wanted to continue sanctions to reach equity. Conservative, pro-White South Africans held to their position that international intervention encouraged hostility and suspicion within South Africa, and that South Africans should be left to negotiate their differences with the minimum of international constraint. This second debate is obviously more complicated, but similar principles revealed by the first debate apply. The case for ongoing, effective sanctions seems clear.

Several principles that pertain to the general use of sanctions emerge from this study and form the basis for a negotiated settlement in South Africa. First, the movement for racial equality in the world is not spent. There have been many reversals, such as the growth of a racial underclass in societies where advances had been made in general race relations, and the brutal suppression of ethnic minorities has become more widespread. At the same time, however, the world has rejected the so-called reform of petty apartheid in South Africa and has insisted on eliminating all racial discrimination.[10]

Second, when the major powers of the world failed to implement economic sanctions, nongovernmental organizations showed themselves capable of mounting strong private sanctions, such as the cultural and economic boycotts represented by the sports and disinvestment campaigns. These have had some significant effects in themselves, as the banning of South Africa from international sport and the pressures placed on banks and major corporations by widespread civic and church campaigns have shown.[11] They have also been the impetus for the policy changes of governments documented in this book.

Third, the world order system is applicable to domestic disputes under certain circumstances and according to international law. As Ved Nanda shows in Chapter 1, the difficulties are immense, and considerable improvement is called for, but the growth of the United Nations and the international legal system has enabled multilateral sanctions to be adopted. The prospects for applying this system to other major human rights violations, despite the reservations of great powers and national sovereignty barriers, have been encouraged by the South African case. Weak unilateral action can lead to powerful collective action by the Security Council.

Fourth, as Haider Ali Khan demonstrates in Chapter 2, sophisticated economic models such as the Social Accounting Matrix (SAM) can be very useful for giving accurate information about the effects of limited international sanctions. Empirical assessment, using multivariate analysis and disaggregated data down to households, can settle the disputes about effectiveness that are inevitably associated with these major international actions. Loopholes do of course exist, but total compliance is not necessary for sanctions to produce significant change in political attitudes.

Fifth, the world is capable of going to an even higher level of comprehensive economic sanctions if that becomes necessary in order to deal with human rights violations of major proportions. In Chapter 3, Sanford Wright shows how this could involve strategic minerals that are not included in existing sanctions. The strategic interests of the United States can be secured against possible retaliation by South Africa because alternative, assured, and economically competitive sources of these minerals can be developed in the United States and the USSR.

Sixth, Stephen Davis argues in Chapter 4 that there has been a gradual shift in U.S. policy to a comprehensive antiapartheid policy by the Bush administration that now includes economic sanctions. These are limited sanctions. The issue remains how to use them effectively in the controversy over the terms of the settlement.

Finally, my own chapter demonstrates how the antiapartheid movement has become a major social movement that has facilitated the implementation of sanctions and progress toward a settlement. This movement has produced effective sanctions that have helped change the political balance inside South Africa and moved the conflict into a negotiation mode. International pressures will need to be applied judiciously and continuously to produce a just settlement.

As David Baldwin and other political economists have suggested, international economic measures are replacing military intervention as means for settling major world conflicts.[12] This challenges previous assumptions about national barriers and the use of force. And it clears the way for a new era of peaceful and just settlement of human rights violations throughout the world.

The conflicts in South Africa are far from settled, but a major milestone appears to have been passed: acceptance by the ruling powers in South Africa that they must adjust to the international economic pressures being placed on them by granting the majority population of Africans the rights of democratic participation. The threat of internal and external upheaval, resulting from the determination of Africans themselves to have their rights, has been no less a decisive reason for the acceptance of this goal. And the struggle itself brings continuous pressure on South African rulers to continue to move toward serious negotiations and make concessions to the majority.

No one can predict when this conflict will end. Nelson Mandela has said it will be soon, but an attempt by the far right to seize power would reverse the progress and could lead to a bloodbath. Even then, however, the final outcome of rule by the majority of South Africa's people would only be postponed. A minority cannot continue to dictate for long. We have passed through a period of reverses, and repression in the world suddenly no longer seems inevitable. Popular democracy continues to sweep through the world, undermining the brutality of dictators and ruling elites.

These chapters were originally a research project of the Consortium on Human Rights Development on the impact of sanctions on South Africa. The contributions of graduate students, especially Timothy Mozia, critiques by NGO leaders and South Africans of various persuasions, and the comments of fellow Africanists have been invaluable over the years in formulating the ideas for this book.

The fast-changing events of South African politics have required us to make some revisions since the initial research began. However, the basic thesis has held up well: international economic intervention is both justified and effective against apartheid. The lessons learned here may be very helpful in a world where military means of intervention are giving way to the use of economic measures to uphold and protect human rights.

NOTES

1. Johan Galtung, "On the Effects of International Sanctions: With Examples from the Case of Rhodesia," *World Politics* 19 (April 1967): 378–416.

2. E. H. Carr, *The Twenty Year Crisis: 1919–1939*. 2d ed. (London: Macmillan, 1975), 109.

3. Quoted in *Africa News* 32, nos. 1/2 (August 1988): 11.

4. Margaret Doxey, *International Sanctions in Contemporary Perspective* (New York: St. Martin's Press, 1987), x.

5. Bruce Russet, "Pearl Harbor: Deterrence Theory and Decision Theory," *Journal of Peace Research* 2 (1967): 89–105.

6. Lord Saint-Brides, "The Lessons of Zimbabwe-Rhodesia," *International Security* 4 (Spring 1980): 177–184.

7. Mohammed Ayoob, ed., *Conflict and Intervention in the Third World* (New York: St. Martin's Press), 224.

8. Jeane J. Kirkpatrick, "Human Rights and Foreign Policy," in *Human Rights in Foreign Policy*, ed. Fred Baumann (Gambier, Ohio: Kenyon College, 1982), 1–11.

9. Robert Edgar, ed., *Sanctioning Apartheid* (Trenton, N.J.: Africa World Press, 1990), 1–19.

10. Paul C. Lauren, *Power and Prejudice: The Politics of Diplomacy and Racial Discrimination* (Boulder, Colo.: Westview Press, 1988), 233.

11. George W. Shepherd, Jr., *Anti-Apartheid: Transnational Conflict and Western Policy in the Liberation of South Africa* (Westport, Conn.: Greenwood, 1977), 140–170.

12. David A. Baldwin, *Economic Statecraft* (Princeton, N.J.: Princeton University Press, 1985), 58.

1

Multilateral Sanctions against South Africa: A Legal Framework for Comprehensive Implementation

Ved P. Nanda

Economic sanctions have become an enduring feature of interstate relations during the twentieth century.[1] States and intergovernmental organizations have frequently used economic sanctions to influence the policies or behavior of a target state within its body politic or in its relations with other actors in the international arena.

Economic sanctions have acquired a special place in state practice in the post–World War II era because of the prohibition against the threat or use of force in international relations as mandated by the U.N. Charter.[2] Thus, as substitutes for armed action, they are likely to supplement other nonviolent pressures on a state, such as diplomatic, ideological (by persuasion and propaganda), and cultural pressures.[3] The impact of these measures will obviously vary, depending upon many factors, including (1) the leverage of the actor or actors imposing sanctions against the target state, (2) the vulnerability of the target state and its capacity to withstand sanctions, and (3) the nature of third states' response in supporting the enforcement of sanctions or in assisting the target state to evade them.

This chapter examines the legal framework of the international sanctions imposed against South Africa, with a special focus on sanctions imposed by the United States. The first section focuses upon the legal bases for such sanctions in the post-U.N. period. This is followed by a brief history of the United Nations' response to South

Africa's violation of its international obligations. Next, the U.S. sanctions against South Africa are discussed in three phases: (1) prior to 1986, (2) under the Comprehensive Anti-Apartheid Act of 1986 (hereinafter CAAA)[4] and (3) post-CAAA developments. These sanctions may be inadequate. Therefore, two additional scenarios are explored: a case for comprehensive and multilateral sanctions against South Africa and a case for humanitarian intervention. In the final section, after an appraisal of the current situation, I offer recommendations for the future.

LEGAL BASES FOR SANCTIONS IN THE POST–U.N. PERIOD

It is commonplace to describe the international legal system as state-based, lacking any centralized authority structures comparable to those in the domestic arena—executive, legislative, and judiciary. Notwithstanding the accuracy of this description, it is undeniable that since 1945 the Security Council of the United Nations has had the authority to undertake mandatory sanctions against a state once the council has determined that the state's activities constitute a threat to the peace, a breach of the peace, or an act of aggression.[5]

While armed action is permissible under the authority of the Security Council,[6] the U.N. Charter also enumerates several nonmilitary coercive measures, including a "complete or partial interruption of economic relations and of rail, sea, air, postal, telegraphic, radio, and other means of communication, and the severance of diplomatic relations."[7]

The collective security system envisioned in the U.N. Charter has never become operational; this, however, by no means detracts from the availability of these measures to the international community. For example, in the following cases the Security Council invoked its powers under chapter 7 of the U.N. Charter to impose sanctions: (1) in 1950 by taking military action in the Korean conflict,[8] (2) in 1966 by imposing mandatory economic sanctions against Southern Rhodesia,[9] and (3) in 1977 by calling for a mandatory arms embargo against South Africa upon determining that South African policies and actions constituted a threat to international peace and security.[10] In addition, the U.N. Charter, in acknowledging the role of regional organizations in the maintenance of international peace and security, authorizes such organizations to impose sanctions.[11]

Pursuant to the recommendations and resolutions of the pertinent organs of the United Nations and regional organizations, legal bases exist for states to undertake coercive economic measures against a state.[12] Finally, unilateral measures against a state are permissible under international law in furtherance of the international law of human rights, especially under the doctrine of humanitarian intervention.[13]

SOUTH AFRICA'S VIOLATIONS OF ITS INTERNATIONAL OBLIGATIONS AND THE UNITED NATIONS

South Africa stands by itself as a special case at the United Nations: it has had the unenviable distinction of being haled before the United Nations as a violator of the generally accepted norms of international law. Evidence of such violations was first presented to the United Nations when the government of India complained to the General Assembly in June 1946 that South Africa was discriminating against Indians residing there.[14] Since then, the United Nations has repeatedly criticized South Africa's policy of apartheid, demanding that it be dismantled and that the people of South Africa be allowed to exercise their right of self-determination.[15] The United Nations has on several occasions condemned South Africa's aggression and policy of destabilization aimed at its neighbors,[16] and has declared South Africa's occupation of Namibia illegal.[17] These considerations have led both the Security Council and the General Assembly to denounce South Africa's activities and impose sanctions against it.[18] The following discussion will recount the pertinent responses by the United Nations.

Treatment of Indians (and Pakistanis) in South Africa, 1946–1962

At the first session of the General Assembly in 1946, the government of India requested the U.N. secretary-general to raise the issue of the treatment of Indians in the Union of South Africa. It sought to place this issue as an agenda item before the General Assembly, suggesting that South Africa's policy of racial discrimination against Indians was "likely to impair friendly relations" between the two states.[19] South Africa invoked article 2, paragraph 7 of the U.N. Charter, which prohibits interference in the domestic affairs of a state.[20] The topic was discussed at a joint committee of the assembly's political and legal committees[21] and at a plenary session of the General Assembly.[22] Following the discussion on December 8, 1946, the General Assembly adopted a resolution by a two-thirds majority, concluding that the relations between these states were "likely to be further impaired" if a satisfactory settlement was not reached.[23] The resolution stated that the treatment of Indians in

South Africa "should be in conformity with the international obligations . . . and the relevant provisions of the Charter."[24]

Over the next 15 years, the General Assembly adopted several
resolutions, urging the parties (which now included Pakistan) to
negotiate a peaceful settlement of the question.[25] In the meantime,
in 1948 the General Assembly adopted the Universal Declaration of
Human Rights,[26] and subsequently established the U.N. Good Offices
Commission to assist the parties in reaching "a satisfactory solution
of the question in accordance with the Purposes and Principles of
the Charter and the Universal Declaration of Human Rights."[27]

South Africa continued to invoke its domestic jurisdiction, thus
declaring U.N. resolutions on the subject unconstitutional and disre-
garding all General Assembly recommendations to abandon its policy
of apartheid and to withhold implementation or enforcement of the
"Group Areas Act" pending conclusion of the negotiations. At its fif-
teenth and sixteenth sessions, the General Assembly noted "with deep
regret" that South Africa had continued to ignore its resolutions.[28]
Eventually, in 1962 the General Assembly consolidated the issue of
discrimination against Indians and Pakistanis with the issue of apartheid, and adopted a combined resolution that requested member
states to take certain measures against South Africa to bring about
a change in its policies of racial discrimination.[29] Subsequently, the
General Assembly considered the question of Indians and Pakistanis
in the broader context of apartheid.

The Question of Apartheid and Race Conflict before the United Nations

In 1952, at the request of thirteen countries, the General Assembly
discussed the issue of apartheid. It was alleged that South Africa's
policy of apartheid was creating a "dangerous and explosive situation,
which constitutes both a threat to international peace and a flagrant
violation of the basic principles of human rights and fundamental
freedoms which are enshrined in the Charter of the United Nations."[30]
The General Assembly adopted a resolution calling upon "all Member
States to bring their policies into conformity with their obligation under
the Charter to promote the observance of human rights and fundamental freedoms," and resolved to establish a commission to study the racial
situation in South Africa.[31] Invoking its domestic jurisdiction rationale, the South African government regarded the General Assembly
resolution as *ultra vires* and refused to cooperate with the commission.
Without South Africa's cooperation, the commission issued three
reports,[32] and the General Assembly at succeeding sessions adopted
resolutions deploring the South African policy of apartheid.[33]

Starting in 1960, when representatives of twenty-nine states asked the Security Council to consider the situation arising out of the Sharpeville massacre, which, they said, was "a situation with grave potentialities for international friction, which endangers the maintenance of international peace and security,"[34] both the Security Council and General Assembly witnessed a shift in the attitude of the remaining few states that had continued to support the South African invocation of its domestic jurisdiction defense.

To illustrate, in 1960 the Security Council called upon South Africa to "abandon its policies of apartheid and racial discrimination."[35] In 1962 the General Assembly adopted a resolution, requesting member states to:

a. break diplomatic relations with South Africa or refrain from establishing them;

b. close their ports to ships flying the South African flag;

c. prohibit their ships from entering South African ports;

d. boycott South African trade; and

e. refuse landing and passage facilities to all aircraft belonging to the government of South Africa or companies registered there.[36]

The resolution also established a special committee against apartheid to review South African racial policies,[37] and requested the Security Council to take action, including sanctions, to ensure South African compliance with U.N. resolutions.[38]

The next year, in August 1963, the Security Council described the situation in South Africa as "seriously disturbing to international peace and security" and called upon all states "to cease forthwith the sale and shipment of arms, ammunition of all types and military vehicles to South Africa."[39] The operative part calling for a boycott of South African trade was not adopted. Subsequently, in December 1963, the Security Council reiterated its call for a ban on arms sales to South Africa, adding to the existing restrictions "the sale and shipment of equipment and materials for the manufacture and maintenance of arms and ammunition in South Africa."[40] It also authorized the secretary-general to appoint a group of experts to examine methods of resolving the situation in South Africa.[41]

In subsequent years, the General Assembly adopted several resolutions condemning South Africa's policy of apartheid and calling for further sanctions.[42] For example, in December 1970 it adopted a resolution urging all states to terminate diplomatic relations and all military, economic, technical, and other cooperation with South Africa, and to "ensure that companies registered in their countries and their nationals comply with the United Nations resolutions on this question."[43] It also requested all states and organizations to "suspend cultural, educational, sporting, and other exchanges" with South Africa and with organizations or institutions in South Africa that practice apartheid.[44] The same year, the Security Council adopted a resolution reiterating its earlier calls for an arms embargo against South Africa, adding that the states should strengthen the arms embargo by ceasing the supply of spare parts used by the South African armed forces and revoking all licenses and military patents granted to the South African government or to South African companies for the manufacture of arms, aircraft, naval craft, or other military vehicles.[45]

It was not, however, until after the Soweto uprising and the enormous casualties suffered at the hands of South African security forces there, and the death in detention of Steve Biko, that the Security Council in November 1977 declared the activities and policies of the South African government to constitute a danger to international peace and security. In a resolution adopted that year, it determined that South Africa's procurement of arms was a "threat to the peace," and imposed the first mandatory arms embargo against South Africa, thereby making it illegal for any member state of the United Nations to sell arms to South Africa.[46] The United States, Britain, and France did not oppose the mandatory sanctions imposed under article 39.

The next Security Council action came in 1985 after the South African regime imposed a state of emergency and its repressive policies resulted in many casualties. The Security Council resolution, adopted in July 1985, urged the U.N. member states to voluntarily impose sanctions against South Africa.[47] The resolution, adopted with the abstention of the United States and the United Kingdom, called for a voluntary cessation of new investment in South Africa, a ban on the sale of Krugerrands, the suspension of export loan guarantees, a ban on nuclear contracts, and an end to the sale of computer equipment that could be used by South African security forces. However, despite all these urgent appeals to impose comprehensive mandatory sanctions against South Africa, including a new oil embargo and strengthened arms embargoes (including an embargo on the supply of equipment and technology to South Africa's oil industry and coal liquefaction project), no efforts have as yet succeeded. For example, in 1987 the General Assembly unsuccessfully urged the Security Council to act immediately under chapter 7 of the U.N. Charter to apply comprehensive and mandatory sanctions against South Africa.[48] At the forty-third session of the General Assembly the assembly decided to hold a special session in 1989 on apartheid and its destructive consequences in southern Africa.[49]

South Africa's apartheid policy must be seen in the context of the emerging international law norms against racial discrimination. A radical transformation in thinking, attitudes, and state practice has occurred in the international arena since 1946, when India brought its complaint against South Africa. The cornerstone of the change is the rapid development of international human rights law.[50] The international community has spoken unequivocally in giving recognition to state obligations regarding nondiscrimination in the U.N. Charter.[51] Among other instruments, the following are pertinent: the Universal Declaration of Human Rights;[52] the International Covenant on Civil and Political Rights;[53] the International Covenant on Economic, Social and Cultural Rights;[54] the 1965 International Convention on the Elimination of All Forms of Racial Discrimination;[55] and the International Convention on the Suppression and Punishment of the Crime of Apartheid.[56]

The norm of nondiscrimination has acquired the status of customary international law, as acknowledged by Judge Tanaka in the *South West Africa* case: "The norm of non-discrimination or non-separation on the basis of race has become a rule of customary international law. . . . This principle [of equality before the law] has become an integral part of the constitutions of most of the civilized countries in the world."[57] The International Law Commission has characterized apartheid as an international crime in its Draft Articles on State Responsibility.[58]

Consequently, the international community is obligated to take appropriate action in response to South Africa's intransigence on these issues.

South Africa's Acts of Aggression and Campaign of Destabilization in the Region

The frontline states—Angola, Botswana, Mozambique, Tanzania, Zambia, and Zimbabwe—contend that South Africa's "campaign of destabilization" in the region cost Pretoria between $10 billion and $60 billion from 1980 to 1987.[59] When the Security Council adopted the mandatory arms embargo resolution in November 1977, it acknowledged "that the military build-up by South Africa and its persistent acts of aggression against the neighboring States seriously disturb the security of those States."[60]

To illustrate, at the General Assembly's thirty-ninth session in 1984, the representative of Angola accused South Africa of "armed aggression, massive invasions, and military occupation of parts of its territory, a sustained battering at the Angolan government, institutions, infrastructure, and people."[61] Earlier, on December 20, 1983, and again on January 6, 1984, the Security Council adopted resolutions demanding that South Africa unconditionally withdraw its military forces occupying Angola.[62] Subsequently, the special committee against apartheid reported to the General Assembly in 1987 that the situation in and around South Africa had markedly deteriorated because of apartheid, "as well as [South Africa's] acts of aggression and destabilization against regional countries."[63]

South Africa, even after its withdrawal from Angola in 1988, continued to support guerrilla movements in its neighboring countries, such as the Mozambique National Resistance Movement and the Lesotho Liberation Army. South Africa reputedly continues to assist the National Union for the Total Independence of Angola (UNITA).[64] It has made several direct military raids on its neighbors, such as in Lesotho in December 1982, in Mozambigue in January 1981 and May 1983, and in Angola in 1981 and 1982. The purpose of such forcible actions has been primarily to put pressure against or to seek the elimination of nationalist activity in South African territory by the South-West African People's Organization (SWAPO) and the African National Congress (ANC).[65] Thus the fact remains that one of the bases for demanding continued sanctions against South Africa remains it acts of aggression and policy of destabilization in the region.

South Africa's Occupation of Namibia, 1945–1990

South Africa's persistent challenge to the United Nations over the status of Namibia (formerly German South-West Africa, brought under South African rule under the League of Nations mandate system) by its refusal to acknowledge Namibia as a trusteeship territory under U.N. supervisory powers, led to the adoption of several resolutions by the General Assembly and the Security Council. Despite this opposition, a recent agreement on independence for Namibia[66] was concluded under the United Nations' auspices. Subsequently, a new constitution was drafted, elections were held, and Namibia earned its place in the family of nations on March 21, 1990.

Starting in 1966, when the General Assembly terminated South Africa's mandate over Namibia,[67] the United Nations considered the continued occupation of Namibia to be illegal. In 1970 the Security Council declared that all acts of the South African government "on behalf of or concerning Namibia after the termination of the mandate are illegal and invalid,"[68] and called upon all states "to refrain from any dealings with the Government of South Africa" that are inconsistent with the declaration.[69]

The next year, at the request of the Security Council, the International Court of Justice gave an advisory opinion, stating that (1) South

Africa was under an obligation to withdraw from Namibia; (2) U.N. members were under obligation to "refrain from any acts and . . . dealings with the Government of South Africa implying recognition of the legality of, or lending support or assistance to South Africa's presence and administration in Namibia; and (3) "it [was] incumbent upon" states that are not U.N. members to provide assistance to these U.N. actions regarding Namibia.[70] Then, in October 1971, the Security Council adopted a resolution expressing agreement with the Court's opinion and called upon all states to comply with and implement the terms of the opinion.[71]

In subsequent years, the General Assembly and the Security Council have adopted numerous resolutions condemning South Africa for its continued illegal presence in Namibia.[72] It is of special note that in 1974 the Council for Namibia enacted a Decree for the Protection of the Natural Resources of Namibia and also decided to establish a research and training institute in Zambia to provide Namibians with the skills necessary to assume responsible positions after independence.[73] Several attempts to impose mandatory sanctions failed; however, in June 1985 the Security Council warned South Africa that its failure to cooperate with the United Nations Transition Assistance Group (UNTAG) in Namibia, which had been established in 1978, would compel the Council to consider the adoption of appropriate measures under the Charter, including those under chapter 7.[74]

In April 1987 the United States, in agreement with South Africa's contention that Cuban troops must be withdrawn from Angola prior to South Africa's withdrawal from Namibia, vetoed a Security Council draft resolution that called for mandatory sanctions against South Africa for its actions in Namibia.[75]

U.S SANCTIONS AGAINST SOUTH AFRICA

The United States and Britain have consistently opposed the United Nations' imposition of mandatory sanctions against South Africa. A mix of domestic and international ideological, political, and economic considerations has resulted in this peculiar foreign policy result. The outcome is especially ironic, for the United States perceives itself not only as a champion of international human rights but also as a staunch proponent of the rule of law in the international arena. There can be little doubt that South Africa's complete disregard for both of these values is at the core of its intransigence.

In addition, the failure of the United States to support mandatory economic sanctions against South Africa on the rationale that such sanctions are likely to be ineffective and futile is neither plausible nor in accordance with its history. The record of U.S. sanctions against Cuba, Libya, Panama, and the Soviet Union, imposed in furtherance of perceived U.S. foreign policy objectives, attests to the continuation of such measures notwithstanding their lack of success. Similarly, the argument that further sanctions will harden whites' resistance, which in President Ronald Reagan's words is not conducive to the "movement toward the resolution of South Africa's political problems in a manner consistent with western values,"[76] has been shown to be incorrect. The underlying assumption of this argument—that diehard whites who have dogmatically demonstrated an inflexible attitude toward peaceful change and the genuine exercise of self-determination in South Africa will act against their best interests in the long run—is unwarranted.

This does not mean, however, that the United States has opposed all sanctions. As the following discussion shows, it has, indeed, joined not only the call for some voluntary sanctions but also for a mandatory arms embargo, and has undertaken these measures on its own accord.

The Pre-1986 Period

During this period, the United States supported the 1963 Security Council decision to impose nonmandatory sanctions against South Africa under chapter 6.[77] It implemented the Security Council decision under the president's authority to limit exports based upon foreign policy considerations.[78] The implementation of the arms embargo, however, was marked by the lack of executive branch commitment, especially during the administrations of Presidents Richard Nixon (who undertook a comprehensive review of U.S. policy toward South Africa) and Ronald Reagan.[79]

Next, the United States implemented the 1977 Security Council resolution, which was adopted in the aftermath of the South African repression in Soweto, to impose a mandatory arms embargo against South Africa.[80] The Departments of State and Commerce promulgated the appropriate regulations.[81]

Then, on September 5, 1985, President Ronald Reagan preempted the Congress, which was about to pass a sanctions bill, by imposing sanctions and invoking the International Emergency Economic Powers Act (IEEPA). These sanctions included a ban on imports of arms from South Africa and the imposition of restrictions on the activities of private financial institutions.[82]

Specifically, all U.S. firms operating in South Africa were advised to adhere to the Sullivan Principles.[83] Additional export restrictions were also imposed, including: (1) a ban on exports of computers and related goods and technology to South African security forces and any governmental entity that assists in the enforcement of apartheid and (2) a ban on all exports of goods and technology that could be used in a South African nuclear facility.[84]

Among import controls, in addition to the prohibition against importation of arms, ammunition, or military vehicles produced in South Africa,[85] was a prohibition against the importation of Kruger-rands.[86] Financial institutions in the United States were also prohibited from extending direct or indirect loans or credits to the South African government or related entities.[87] The Comprehensive Anti-Apartheid Act of 1986[88] superseded these limited sanctions.

The Comprehensive Anti-Apartheid Act of 1986

The Comprehensive Anti-Apartheid Act (CAAA) became law on October 2, 1986, despite the hostility toward it and veto of this legislation by President Reagan. The purpose of the CAAA was to coordinate U.S. actions in the context of "a comprehensive and complete framework," to help "bring an end to apartheid in South Africa and lead to the establishment of a nonracial, democratic form of Government."[89] Specific objectives of the act included the repeal of the state of emergency, the release of Nelson Mandela and other political prisoners, the free exercise of political association and political expression, the establishment of a timetable for the abolition of apartheid laws, negotiations between representatives of all racial groups concerning the future political system of South Africa, and an end to armed aggression against the black-ruled neighboring states of southern Africa.[90]

The CAAA attempts to employ a "graduated response" in order to reflect any progress or setbacks in the achievement of the stated objectives.[91] The act also seeks to encourage the African National Congress to suspend terrorist activities, make public commitment to a "democratic" South Africa, enter into negotiation with the government, and reconsider its ties to the South African Communist Party.[92]

Substantively, the act provides first for measures for assistance to the victims of apartheid. Such assistance includes education, legal aid, and political, economic, and diplomatic pressure on the South African government.[93]

In addition, the CAAA prohibits the importation of certain South African commodities into the United States. Restricted commodities include gold coins, nuclear items and arms (previously restricted by the president), uranium, coal, steel, iron, textiles, and sugar.[94] All imports from South African parastatal organizations are banned except for strategic minerals and publications.[95]

The act also prohibits certain U.S. exports to South Africa. Areas covered by the export restrictions include (1) computer exports to the South African government or other agencies enforcing apartheid; (2) nuclear trade with South Africa; (3) the export of certain arms to South Africa; and (4) the export of petroleum to South Africa by a person or entity subject to the jurisdiction of the United States.[96]

Air traffic between the two countries is prohibited. In addition, certain contacts with the South African government are prohibited, including military cooperation, some intelligence cooperation, U.S. government funding for South African trade, U.S. government procurement in South Africa, and U.S. government funding for the promotion of tourism in South Africa.[97]

One of the more effective provisions of the CAAA terminates the tax treaty between South Africa and the United States that had prevented "double-taxation" of multinational businesses.[98] Another provision, aimed at discouraging private business dealings with South Africa, banned all new investments in South Africa, except for investments in firms owned by black South Africans.[99] Those U.S. companies continuing to do business in South Africa and employing more than 25 people were required to take steps to implement the Sullivan Principles.[100] American financial institutions were also prohibited from making loans to the South African government or any of its agencies or corporations, as well as from receiving funds for deposit from any South African government entity.[101]

In the case of violation of any of the provisions of the CAAA, substantial penalties apply. These include individual fines of up to $50,000 and 10 years imprisonment and corporate fines of up to one million dollars.[102]

The CAAA also threatens to impose further sanctions if the situation in South Africa does not indicate "substantial progress."[103] These stated measures include a ban on South African diamonds and strategic minerals, a prohibition on the deposit of funds in U.S. banks by South African nationals, and a ban on military assistance to those nations that assist South Africa in circumventing the international arms embargo.[104] These measures are to be implemented, however, only if the president determines that South Africa has not taken substantial steps to dismantle the system of apartheid. To date, both president Reagan and Bush have determined that further sanctions would not be helpful.

Recent Developments

The imposition of additional sanctions, therefore, has been the subject of proposed legislation for the last several sessions of Congress.

The 1988 proposed legislation failed to be enacted into law. In 1989, several bills were introduced into the 101st Congress in an attempt to strengthen the existing regime of sanctions,[105] but again were not enacted.

Both Senate Bill 507 and House Bill 21 provide for similar additional sanctions. These would include a prohibition on virtually all private investment in South Africa by U.S. nationals, a prohibition on virtually all noncharitable exports of goods or technology to South Africa from the United States, and the banning of most South African exports to the United States, except certain strategic minerals.[106] The bills would also strengthen sanctions against nuclear assistance to South Africa, and the prohibitions against intelligence and military cooperation with South Africa.[107] In addition, the bills forbid the transport of oil to South Africa on U.S. registered or owned ships under penalty of losing lease privileges under various acts governing mineral and oil explorations on U.S. lands and the U.S. continental shelf.[108]

The bills also call for the commencement of negotiations to implement a multilateral regime of sanctions against South Africa and give the president the power to ban imports into the United States from foreign firms that take significant commercial advantage of U.S. sanctions against South Africa.[109]

THE CASE FOR COMPREHENSIVE MULTILATERAL SANCTIONS

The steps taken by the de Klerk government to dismantle apartheid are encouraging, but they fall far short of meeting the U.N.'s criteria for abolishing racial discrimination and ensuring democratic representation of the African majority. Additional sanctions may well be necessary. The question is, what form should they take?

While the history of various sanctions against South Africa shows some progress, they have as yet been ineffective due to flaws in the format or implementation of the measures. Since the early 1960s there has been a voluntary arms embargo against South Africa, authorized by the U.N. Security Council.[110] The United States has complied with this embargo since 1964,[111] and the embargo was made mandatory by the Security Council in 1977.[112] Various loopholes have existed in the U.S. scheme; the divided responsibility for enforcement in the U.S. bureaucracy and the relatively low priority given to the embargo (in comparison to embargoes against other nations, such as the Soviet Union) have made the arms ban ineffective.[113] Further, the gradual evolution of the ban from voluntary to mandatory permitted the South African government to not only find alternative suppliers willing to deal with it, but also allowed the South African arms industry to achieve a degree of self-sufficiency. Similar problems are likely to arise with any sanctions that are not multilateral.

An additional problem is the limited character of the sanctions. This can be illustrated by viewing South Africa's mineral exports. In the CAAA, Congress permitted the president to prepare a list of "strategic minerals" that are exempted from the ban on imports from South African parastatals.[114]

The executive has formulated a broad definition of "strategic minerals," thereby exempting a greater number of South African exports than the Congress probably intended.[115]

Definitional problems often plague sanctions that are non-comprehensive. Further, since most sanctions must be multilateral to be effective, the problem of defining a concept such as "strategic minerals" for many nations is likely to provide differing definitions and more loopholes that will erode the efficacy of sanctions.

Even when a ban appears complete on its face, such as the prohibition against U.S. export of petroleum products to South Africa, loopholes have been created due to interpretation. An example of this is the executive's determination that petrochemicals are not "petroleum products" and are not subject to the ban.[116] The ban has also been interpreted not to prohibit re-export of the petroleum from third countries to South Africa.[117]

The non-comprehensive nature of the CAAA is perhaps best illustrated by the ban on new investments. This ban is clearly a step below divestment and the difficulty in determining what a new investment is, as well as several legislative exceptions to the ban, have severely weakened the effect of this prohibition. For example, reinvestment of profits in existing operations is permitted, as well as several other types of financial transfers necessary to maintain existing operations.[118]

The technical issues will not be explored here, but it should be noted that the non-comprehensive nature of the sanctions creates a degree of ambiguity in what investments are permitted under the CAAA. It could be argued that such ambiguity permits a degree of flexibility to avoid unintended consequences, and that in many ambiguous situations a prudent business person would resolve the ambiguity in favor of non-investment in response to the potentially large penalties that may be imposed. However, such an argument assumes that there exists a commitment to enforce penalties against violators. Such a regime of vigorous enforcement has not been in evidence as of this date.

This discussion has thus far demonstrated that previous attempts at unilateral, non-comprehensive sanctions have not been successful. While there are grounds for optimism, as argued elsewhere in this book, it is too early to determine the effectiveness of the 1986 CAAA.

Further sanctions may be added through amendments as necessary. It should be noted that the act contains many of the defects that were evident in earlier failed attempts to impose an arms embargo against South Africa. One significant improvement is the encouragement of multilateral initiatives in the CAAA.

The central lesson to be learned from the South African experience is that the imposition of broad multilateral sanctions is essential if the policies or conduct of a recalcitrant state such as South Africa are to be fully affected.

As discussed earlier, ample bases under international law exist for such action. To recapitulate, these bases include South Africa's apartheid policy, its resistance to self-determination, its aggression against neighboring countries, and its Namibia policy. As noted, even though the Namibian question is settled, there remain appropriate legal bases for such sanctions.

In addition, South Africa's apartheid policy arguably presents the international community with a challenge of such magnitude that the use of humanitarian intervention should be considered an appropriate response.

HUMANITARIAN INTERVENTION AND SOUTH AFRICA

The Doctrine of Humanitarian Intervention

Humanitarian intervention is defined here as the use of force by states in another state to protect basic human rights of individuals and groups, including nationals, who are deprived of such rights.[119] International lawyers are divided on the validity of humanitarian intervention in the post-U.N. era.[120] The divergence of opinions stems from the varying interpretations of the U.N. Charter provision that prohibits "the threat or use of force" by member states "against the territorial integrity or political independence of any State."[121]

I have argued elsewhere that notwithstanding the ongoing debate on whether humanitarian intervention has survived the Charter prohibition as customary international law, "in certain limited, extraordinary situations, [where] gross and persistent violations of basic human rights prevail in a nation, intervention by a group of states or even by a single state is justified under international law."[122]

The prerequisites for such unilateral action are: (1) collective action under the auspices of the United Nations or regional organizations is not feasible, and (2) an ongoing or imminent threat to basic human rights exists. The nature and scope of intervention must also meet the traditional test of proportionality: the force used must be proportionate to the nature and extent of the violations and the remedy required to correct such violations. Also, forcible intervention can be justified only as a last resort, when the intervening state or states have exhausted all peaceful means (the only exception being that peaceful means are not likely to succeed). Peaceful means include diplomatic, ideological, and economic activities. Finally, the intervening state (or states) remains accountable to the international community for its activities; it must render prompt, thorough, and complete reports of its action to appropriate U.N. and regional organizations.

APPRAISAL AND RECOMMENDATIONS

Despite some change, South Africa continues to present the world community with a grave challenge. Although the United States has taken a significant and symbolic initiative in the sanctions debate over South Africa's apartheid system, the CAAA and the subsequent amendments are neither comprehensive nor multilateral. Neither of the 1989 bills[123] passed Congressional and White House hurdles, and it is unlikely that any further U.S. sanctions will be realistically considered in the near future. Thus, an appropriate question is, what next?

A legal framework exists within which the United States regulates its economic relationships with South Africa. The desirable next steps are to bring the sanctions into the international arena through multilateral action and to expand the sanctions through political tools and additional economic weapons.

Multilateral, if not universal, action needs to be taken if the sanctions are to prove effective. Cooperative agreements are essential to overcoming the problems of third-party circumvention, particularly by major trading partners of the United States. Similar arrangements are essential to address the two other stumbling blocks, the one related to strategic minerals and national security within the context of a superpower arms race, and the other to interdependence of a global investment community with multinational private entities. Also, the problem of the "frontline states" could be substantially cleared through cooperative agreements between the members of the world community wishing to force the South African government to change, essentially to reform itself out of power.

Although Congress took the initial steps with the promulgation of CAAA in 1986, any further efforts to address the issue on an international level will have to be made by the executive. This is unlikely because President Bush is inclined to cut back sanctions rather than to expand them. The basis of any success will have to be an inherent willingness of all parties to fight against apartheid. There can be no better incentive, nor can the United States expect to enforce multilateral sanctions through penalties against its friends, allies, and trading partners. As "clear" as the moral issue of apartheid appears to any reasonable person, the international system has not yet gone beyond the steps of condemnation and disapproval.

Many questions arise about any proposal for a multilateral approach toward South Africa. The basic question is, under what structure? If we return to the context of sanctions under the aegis of the United Nations, clearly the United States, as well as all members of the Security Council, should be an integral part. The United Nations is the only "universal " body in the international community that could push through initiatives that carry the moral voice of all peoples, as well as being comprehensive and universal. Third-party circumvention problems would be best approached through this channel. The subject of strategic minerals and their impact on the industry and national security of member states could also be addressed appropriately through the United Nations under cooperative agreements. This will require a concerted effort by permanent members of the Security Council.

On the other hand, issues related to foreign investment are probably not conducive to a U.N. approach. Other important players in this area, including banks and multinational corporations, would have to be involved. Here, each individual state is going to have to make its own decisions and sacrifices. The emphasis here has to be placed on peer pressure toward implementing sanctions.

After four decades of various efforts against apartheid the world community finds itself unable to fully get rid of this evil. The failure lies not in the inadequacy of legal bases to undertake effective measures against South Africa, but in the lack of political will and vision on the part of western democracies. Accordingly, a strong U.S. leadership, accompanied by British support, is essential for the imposition of strong multilateral and effective sanctions against South Africa.

NOTES

I gratefully acknowledge the research assistance of Jeffrey Maddox, editor of the *Denver Journal of International Law and Policy*, and David Penna, J.D., University of Denver College of Law and a Ph.D. student at the University of Denver Graduate School of International Studies.

1. Extensive literature exists on the subject. See e.g., D. Baldwin, *Economic Statecraft* (1985) [hereinafter Baldwin]; B. Carter, *International Economic Sanctions* (1988); M. Doxey, *International Sanctions in Contemporary Perspective* (1987); G. Hufbauer & J. Schott, *Economic Sanctions Reconsidered* (1985); D. Losman, *International Economic Sanctions: The Cases of*

Cuba, Israel, and Rhodesia (1979); and P. Wallensteen and M. Nincic, eds., *Dilemmas of Economic Sanctions* (1983).

2. Article 2, para. 4 of the U.N. Charter reads: "All Members shall refrain in their international relations from the threat or use of force against the territorial integrity or political independence of any state, or in any other manner inconsistent with the Purposes of the United Nations."

3. See e.g., Baldwin, 13–14.

4. Comprehensive Anti-Apartheid Act of 1986, Pub. L. No. 99-440, 100 Stat. 1086–1116, codified at 22 U.S.C. Sec. 5001–5016 (Supp. IV 1986).

5. See U.N. Charter art. 39. See also id. chs. VI, VII.

6. See U.N. Charter art. 42.

7. Id. art. 41.

8. See S.C. Res. 82 of June 25, 1950, 5 U.S. SCOR, Resolutions and Decisions at 4 (1950); S.C. Res. 83 of June 27, 1950, 5 U.N. SCOR, Resolution and Decisions at 5 (1950); S.C. Res. 84 of July 7, 1950, 5 U.N. SCOR Resolutions and Decisions at 5 (1950). For a review of the U.N. efforts in Korea from 1948 to 1953, see Goodrich, "Korea: Collective Measures against Aggression," 494 *International Conciliation* 129 (1953).

9. See S.C. Res. 232, 21 U.N. SCOR, Resolutions and Decisions at 7 (1966).

10. See S.C. Res. 408, 32 U.N. SCOR, Resolutions and Decisions at 5–6 (1977).

11. See U.N. Charter art. 52, para. 1, which provides:

Nothing in the present Charter precludes the existence of regional arrangements or agencies for dealing with such matters relating to the maintenance of international peace and security as are appropriate for regional action, provided that such arrangements or agencies and their activities are consistent with the Purposes and Principles of the United Nations.

12. U.N. Charter ch. VII.

13. See infra notes 119–122 and accompanying text.

14. See infra notes 19–24 and accompanying text.

15. See infra notes 30–49 and accompanying text.

16. See infra notes 59–65 and accompanying text.

17. See infra notes 66–75 and accompanying text.

18. See infra notes 42–49 and accompanying text.

19. See Letter from the Indian Delegation to the U.N. Secretary General, June 22, 1946, 1 (pt. 2) U.N. GAOR, Jt. Comm. of Comms. 1 & 6, at 52–53, U.N. Doc. 1/149 (1946). India invoked articles 10 and 14 of the U.N. Charter.

20. See Memorandum by the Government of South Africa, Oct. 31, 1946, 1 (pt. 2) U.N. GAOR, Jt. Comm. of Comms. 1 & 6 at 110–111, U.N. Doc. 1/167 (1946).

21. See 1 (pt. 2) U.N. GAOR, Jt. Comm. of Comms. 1 & 6, at 1–51 (1946).

22. See 1 U.N. GAOR (pt. 2), Plenary 1006–61 (1946).

23. See G.A. Res. 44 (1), 1 (pt. 2) U.N. GAOR, Resolutions at 69, U.N. Doc. A/64/Add. 1 (1946).

24. See id., operative para. 2.

25. For a brief history, see L. Sohn and T. Buergenthal, *International Protection of Human Rights* 583–587 (1973), [hereinafter Sohn & Buergenthal].

26. G.A. Res. 217, 3 (pt. 1) U.N. GAOR, Resolutions at 71–77, U.N. Doc. A/810 (1948).

27. See G.A. Res. 615, 7 U.N. GAOR, Supp. (No. 20) at 8, U.N. Doc. A/2361 (1952). See also G.A. Res. 919, 10 U.N. GAOR, Supp. (No. 19) at 8, U.N. Doc. A/3116 (1955); G.A. Res. 1179, 12 U.N. GAOR, Supp. (No. 18), at 8, U.N. Doc A/3805 (1957); G.A. Res. 1460, 14 U.N. GAOR, Supp. (No. 16) at 8, U.N. Doc. A/4354 (1959).

28. See G.A. Res. 1597, 15 U.N. GAOR, Supp. (16A) at 5, U.N. Doc. A/4684/Add. 1 (1961); G.A. Res. 1662, 16 U.N. GAOR, Supp. (No. 17) at 10, U.N. Doc. A/5100 (1962–63).

29. See G.A. Res. 1761, 17 U.N. GAOR, Supp. (No. 17) at 9–10, U.N. Doc. A/5217 (1962).

30. For the text of the letter, see 7 U.N. GAOR, Annexes,No. 66, at 11–3, U.N. Doc. A/2183 (1952).

31. See G.A. Res. 616 (VII) A and B, 7 U.N. GAOR, Supp. (No. 20) at 8–9, U.N. Doc. A/2361 (1952).

32. For a summary report, see Sohn and Buergenthal at 641–670.

33. For a brief report, see id. at 663–664, 668–672.

34. See 15 U.N., SCOR, Supp. for Jan.–Mar. 1960, at 58, U.N. Doc. S/4279 & Add. 1 (1960).

35. See 15 U.N. SCOR, Supp. for April–June 1960, at 1, U.N. Doc. S/4300 (1960).

36. See G.A. Res. 1761 (XVII), 17 U.N. GAOR, Supp. (No. 17) at 9–10, U.N. Doc. A/5217 (1962) (operative para. 4).

37. See id. operative para. 5.

38. See id. operative para. 8.

39. S.C. Res. 181, 18 U.N. SCOR, Resolutions and Decisions at 7, U.N. Doc. S/INF/18/ Rev. 1 (1963).

40. S.C. Res. 182, 18 U.N. SCOR, Resolutions and Decisions at 8–10, U.N. Doc. S/INF/18/Rev. 1 (1983).

41. Id. operative para. 6.

42. See generally Sohn & Buergenthal at 720–722, 731–735.

43. See G.A. Res. 2671F, 25 U.N. GAOR, Supp. (No. 28) at 34, U.N. Doc. A/8028 (1970).

44. See id. For the text of several resolutions on the subject, see 25 U.N. GAOR, Supp. (No. 28) 31–34, U.N. Doc. A/8028 (1970).

45. See S.C. Res. 282, 25 U.N. SCOR, Resolutions and Decisions at 12 (1970).

46. See S.C. Res. 418, 32 U.N. SCOR Resolutions and Decisions at 5 (1977).

47. See S.C. Res. 569, adopted on July 26, 1985.

48. See 25 *UN Chronicle*, No. 1, March 1988, at 61, 63.

49. See 26 *UN Chronicle*, No. 1, March 1989, at 49.

50. See e.g., M. McDougal, H. Lasswell, and L. Chen, *Human Rights and World Public Order* (New Haven: Yale University Press, 1980); A. H. Robertson, *Human Rights in the World* 2d ed. (Manchester, England: Manchester University Press, 1982).

51. See e.g., U.N. Charter arts. 1 (3), 55, 56.

52. See G.A. Res. 217 A (III), at 71, U.N. Doc. A/810 (1948). Article 7 reads, in part: "All are equal before the law and are entitled without any discrimination to the equal protection of the law."

53. See G.A. Res. 2200, 21 U.N. GAOR Supp. (No. 16) at 52, U.N. Doc. A/6316 (1966).

54. See G.A. Res. 2200, 21 U.N. GAOR Supp. (No. 16) at 49, U.N. Doc. A/6316 (1966).

55. See 660 U.N.T.S. 195 (1969).

56. See G.A. Res. 3068, 28 U.N. GAOR Supp. (No. 30) at 75, U.N. Doc. A/9030 (1973).

57. See South West Africa Case (Ethiopia v. South Africa; Libya v. South Africa) Second Phase, (1966) I.C.J. Rep. 4, 293–299 (Tanaka J., dissenting).

58. See Art. 19, which reads in part:

> 2. An internationally wrongful act which results from the breach by a State of an international obligation so essential for the protection of fundamental interests of the international community that its breach is recognized as a crime by that community as a whole, constitutes an international crime.

> 3. Subject to paragraph 2, on the basis of the rules of international law in force, an international crime may result, *inter alia* from:

> (c) a serious breach on a widespread scale of an international obligation of essential importance for safeguarding the human being, such as those prohibiting slavery, genocide, and apartheid.

International Law Commission Draft Articles on State Responsibility, report of the International Law Commission to the General Assembly, art. 19, U.N. Doc. A/31/10, reprinted in 2 *Y.B. International Law Commission* 73, 95 (1976).

59. See L. Junggven, *EC to Meet Frontline States for South African Talks*, Reuters, April 18, 1989, AM Cycle.

60. S.C. Res. 418, 32 U.N. SCOR, Resolutions and Decisions at 5 (1977).

61. Quoted in 21 *UN Chronicle*, No. 9, at 21 (1984).

62. For a report on the discussion in the Security Council and the resolutions, see id., No. 2, at 59 (1984).

63. 25 *UN Chronicle*, No. 1, March 1988, at 62.

64. See generally, I. W. Zartman, *Ripe for Revolution* 152–219 (1988).

65. See id. at 196.

66. On negotiations leading to the agreement, see 25 *UN Chronicle*, No. 4, Dec. 1988, at 28–29.

67. Pursuant to G.A. Res. 2145, 21 U.N. GAOR, Supp. (No. 16) at 2, U.N. Doc. A/6316 (1966). The Security Council adopted Resolution 264 on March 20, 1969, recognizing the termination of the mandate and calling upon the Government of South Africa to withdraw from the territory.

68. See S.C. Res. 276, 25 U.N. SCOR, Resolutions and Decisions at 1, U.N. Doc. S/INF/276 (1970) (operative para. 2).

69. Id. operative para. 6.

70. See Legal Consequences for States of the Continued Presence of South Africa in Namibia . . ., (1971) I.C.J. Rep. 16.

71. See S.C. Res. 301, 26 U.N. SCOR, Resolutions and Decisions at 7, U.N. Doc. S/26/301.

72. For a chronology of U.N. actions in Namibia, see 23 *UN Chronicle*, No. 5, at 25 (1986).

73. See id.

74. See S.C. Res. 566 of June 19, 1985, reported in id.

75. See *N.Y. Times*. April 10, 1987, at A6.

76. *Progress Toward Ending System of Apartheid* 6 (House Doc. 101–5, 101st Cong., 1st Sess., GPO, 1989)—Communication from President Reagan transmitting the second annual report on the extent to which significant progress has been made toward ending apartheid in South Africa.

77. See S.C. Res. 181, 18 U.N. SCOR, Resolutions and Decisions at 7 (1963).

78. See the Export Administration Act, 50 U.S.C. app. Sec. 2401–2410 (1982) and Supp. III 1985. For the 1949 Export Control Act, see 50 U.S.C. app. Sec. 2021–2032 (1964).

79. See generally Butcher, "The Unique Nature of Sanctions against South Africa, and Resulting Enforcement Issues," 19 *N.Y.J. International & Pol.* 821, 829, 843–845 (1987). In 1985, some of the earlier regulations promulgated during the Reagan administration, which had narrowed the export controls against South Africa, were significantly modified pursuant to President Reagan's Exec. Order. 12, 532. See infra notes 82–84.

80. See S.C.Res. 418, 32 U.N. SCOR, Resolutions and Decisions at 5 (1977).

81. See 15 C.F.R. Sec. 371.2, 373.1 (1987).

82. See Exec. Order No. 12,532, C.F.R. 387 (1986), 50 Fed. Reg. 175 (1985) [hereinafter Exec. Order 12,532].

83. See Exec. Order 12,532 Sec. 2.

84. Id. Sec. 1. For the implementing regulations, see 50 Fed. Reg. 47,363 (1985). There are certain exceptions to the export of goods and technology that might be used in a South Africa nuclear facility.

85. See Exec. Order 12,532 Sec. 1 (d).

86. See Exec. Order 12,535, 3 C.F.R. 393 (1986).

87. See id. Sec. 1.

88. Pub. L. No. 99–440, 100 Stat. 1086, codified at 22 U.S.C. Sec. 5001–5016 (Supp. IV 1986 [hereinafter CAAA].

89. Id. at Sec. 5002.

90. Id. at Sec. 5011 (b).

91. Id. at Sec. 5011 (c).

92. Id. at Sec. 5012.

93. Id. at Sec. 5013.

94. Id. at Secs. 5051, 5052, 5059, 5070 and 5073.

95. Id. at Sec. 5053.

96. Id. at Secs. 5054, 5057, 5067 and 5071.

97. Id. at Secs. 5064–5066, 5072–5072a.

98. Id. at Sec. 5063.

99. Id. at Sec. 5060.

100. Id. at Secs. 5034 and 5035.

101. Id. at Secs. 5055 and 5058.

102. Id. Sec. 5113.

103. Id. at Sec. 5091.

104. Id.

105. In the House, H.R. 636 and H.R. 21 were introduced; in the Senate S.507 was introduced. Additionally, Senator Jesse Helms introduced S.522 in an attempt to repeal the CAAA.

106. See e.g., Senate Bill 507, 101st Cong., 1st Sess. (March 3, 1989), Secs. 101–102, 201.

107. Id. at Sec. 104–105.

108. Id. at Sec. 111.

109. Id. at Sec. 202.

110. Sec. Council Res. 181, 18 U.N.S.C.O.R. 7, U.N. Doc. S/INF/18/Rev. (1963).

111. See Export Control Act of 1949, 50 U.S.C. app. Secs. 2021–2032 (1964).

112. Sec. Council Res. 418, 32 U.N.S.C.O.R. 5, U.N. Doc. S/INF/33 (1977).

113. See Comment, "The United States Arms Embargo Against South Africa: An Analysis of the Laws, Regulations, and Loopholes," 12 *Yale J. International Law*, 133 (1987).

114. CAAA, Supra note Sec. 5053.

115. See Southern Africa Project, *Implementation of the Comprehensive Anti-Apartheid Act of 1986*, (Washington, D.C.: Lawyers Comm. for Civil Rights under Law, 1988) at 24–26.

116. Id. at 66.

117. Id. at 65.

118. See Id. at 83–101.

119. On humanitarian intervention, see generally F. R. Teson, *Humanitarian Intervention* (Dobbs Ferry, N.Y.: Transnational Publishers, 1988); Richard Lillich, ed., *Humanitarian Intervention and the United Nations* (Charlottesville: University Press of Virginia, 1973); M. Bazler, "Re-examining the Doctrine of Humanitarian Intervention in Light of the Atrocities in Kampuchea and Ethiopia," 23 *Stanford Journal of International Law* 547 (1987); Clark, "Humanitarian Intervention: Help to Your Friends and State Practice," 13 *Georgia Journal International and Comp. Law* L. 211 (1983) (Supp.); Fonteyne, "Forcible Self-Help by States to Protect Human Rights: Recent Views from the United Nations," in Lillich, ed., *Humanitarian Intervention and the United Nations*, 197; Franck and Rodley, "After Bangladesh: the Law of Humanitarian Intervention by Military Force," 67 *A.J.I.L.* 275 (1973); Green, "Humanitarian Intervention—1976 Version," 24 *Chitty's Law Journal* 217 (1976); Jhabvala, "Unilateral Humanitarian Intervention and International Law," 21 *Indian Journal International Law* 208 (1981); Lillich, "Humanitarian Intervention: A Reply to Ian Brownlie and a Plea for Constructive Alternatives," in J. N. Moore, ed., *Law and Civil War in the Modern World*, 229 (1974); Reisman, "Coercion and Self-Determination: Construing Article 2 (4)," 78 *A.J.I.L.* 642 (1984); Farer, "Intervention and Human Rights: The Latin American Context," 12 *Calif. West.*

International Law Journal 503 (1982); Nanda, "The United States Armed Intervention in Grenada—Impact on World Order," 14 *Calif. W. International Law Journal* 395 (1984); Nanda, "Humanitarian Military Intervention," 23 *Worldview*, October 1980, at 23; Schachter, "The Right of States to Use Armed Force," 82 *Michigan Law Review* 1920 (1984); Schachter, "In Defense of International Rules on the Use of Force," 53 *University of Chicago Law Review* 113 (1985); Verwey, "Humanitarian Intervention under International Law," 23 *Netherlands International Law Review* 357 (1985).

120. Illustrative of the divergence of opinions are I. Brownlie, "Humanitarian Intervention," in Moore, ed., *Law and Civil War in the Modern World* 219 (1974); and R. Lillich, "Humanitarian Intervention: A Reply to Ian Brownlie and a Plea for Constructive Alternatives," Ibid., at 229.

121. See art. 2, para. 4 of the U.N. Charter.

122. See Nanda, "Humanitarian Military Intervention," supra note 119, at 23.

123. See supra notes 105–109.

2

Multiplier and Structural Path Analysis of Trade Sanctions

Haider Ali Khan

In this chapter the question of the economic impact of sanctions is taken up in an economy-wide setting. The proponents as well as the opponents in the sanction debate agree that this is an important issue. Nevertheless, only recently have there been the beginnings of studies attempting to estimate the impacts throughout the South African economy.[1] In the following pages I present analyses based on a fixed-price, multisectoral model for South Africa. For empirical estimations I have used the recently available Social Accounting Matrix for South Africa.[2]

The issue of trade sanctions has attracted increasing attention recently. This is for two reasons. First of all, the mixed results of investment sanctions undertaken so far (Khan 1989)[3] have led to a reemphasis on trade sanctions. Secondly, and related to the first point, the relative neglect of trade sanctions calls for new approaches and analyses at this juncture. In what follows I first outline an approach about how to think about sanctions and their effects in general. Then I use the recently developed Social Accounting Matrix (SAM) approach to the analysis of trade sanctions in order to estimate as a first approximation the impacts of export sanctions. I go one step further than existing work by decomposing the SAM-based fixed price multipliers. This is done by using the method of structural path analysis. I finish with some thoughts on what we can conclude from such an analysis as to the future behavior of South Africa. I also discuss how the present framework can be extended to estimate the impact of trade sanctions on Southern African economies as a whole.

ARE SANCTIONS EFFECTIVE POLICY INSTRUMENTS?

The literature on sanctions is replete with claims about their *ineffectiveness*. However, it is usually not recognized that sanctions may be ineffective (or effective, as proponents of sanctions claim) in at least two different ways. First, they may be ineffective in not being enforceable. This is a serious issue since what cannot be enforced cannot have any effects whatsoever, except perhaps accidental and usually unintended ones. However, claiming that sanctions are not enforceable at all is just as extreme a position as the opposite naive assumption of complete enforceability. Later in this chapter I overcome this problem by postulating an effectiveness parameter for sanctions that can vary between 0 (completely ineffective, in the sense defined above) and 1 (completely effective).[4] The second way to argue that sanctions are ineffective is to point out that they very seldom achieve their goals. The problem with this view is that the goals are usually defined very unrealistically. David Baldwin points out that sanctions are often supposed to have such goals as:

Getting Italy to abandon its invasion of Ethiopia after it had already begun. Getting Castro to step down. Getting Israel to abolish itself. Getting Rhodesian whites to accept majority rule. Getting the Soviet Union to change its political system. Promoting economic development and democracy in countries that have never known either. Getting the United States to change its policy of support for Israel in response to a public demand based on an oil embargo.[5]

I have proposed that the effectiveness of sanctions be judged by looking not at these and similar lofty goals but at intermediate effects. Such effects as an increase in the willingness of a recalcitrant country in the international system to negotiate I have called induced effects of sanctions. Schematically, the process for sanctions against apartheid may be described as in Figure 1.

Assuming that sanctions have some effects, how are we to gauge those effects? In the following section I attempt to deal with this question for the case of trade sanctions.

THE SAM-BASED APPROACH TO ESTIMATE THE IMPACTS OF TRADE SANCTIONS

The Social Accounting Matrix based approach to analyze the effects of export sanctions is the result of my work in this area during the

Figure 1
Political and Economic Impacts of the Sanctions Model

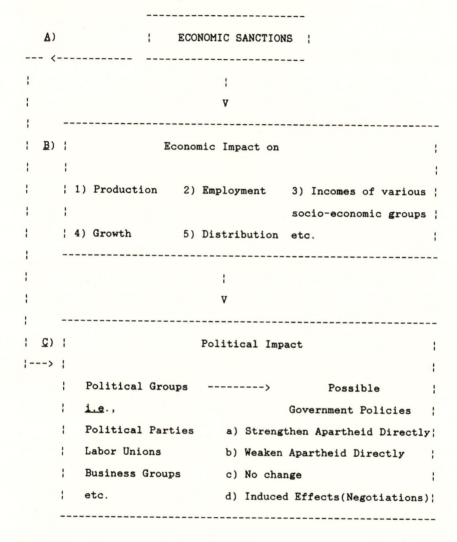

last three years. It is a natural and logical extension of the input-output based approach of some other authors such as Spandau and Richardson.[6] I will first offer a synopsis of SAM and the modeling strategy based on it and then describe in detail empirical results obtained from the only available South African SAM.

The SAM can be thought of as a convenient way of describing empirically the circular flow of income in society. This is illustrated in

Figure 2, which is a schematic diagram for the South African SAM. Incomes are received by rows from the columns. Each account receives as well as spends money. Therefore, the SAM conceptually has to be a square matrix. The accounting identity, expenditures = receipts—sometimes called the fundamental (and perhaps the only) law in economics—has to be satisfied for each row and column. This imposes a very stringent consistency requirement.

In the South African SAM there are 24 production activities, capital, 40 different types of labor, 28 different types of households, and several other accounts as well (see Figure 2). There are several features that are of immediate relevance to the modeling of the impact of sanctions. First of all, the detail on the production side allows one to single out important sectors such as gold or agriculture for consideration. The detail on the labor side is extremely valuable since in most discussions labor is assumed to be homogeneous, differentiated by race only. This is obviously not true if one looks at the tenfold division of labor types within each of the racial categories. Finally, households are also classified by race and income categories. It could have been desirable to have capital disaggregated as well. Unfortunately, this could not be done given the lack of data on ownership of capital.

The modeling of export embargoes is described in detail elsewhere.[7] Briefly, export sanctions lead to a fall in demand for the particular sector that has been sanctioned. Through a combination of direct and indirect effects this leads ultimately to a fall in *aggregate* demand that is distributed among many sectors, including the original one, calling for economy-wide adjustments. These changes can be estimated by computing a *set* of fixed price multipliers. Table 1 gives a set of these multipliers for 10 sectors of the South African economy. Each multiplier can be interpreted as a decline in the income of a particular row when sanctions lead to a unit decrease in demand for the product indicated by the column. I now turn to a discussion of the impact of export sanctions, judging from trends in the actual data. (See tables in the appendix at the end of this chapter for trade data for South Africa.)

Fixed Price Multipliers and Sanctions

Turning now to the issue of actually estimating the effect of export sanctions, the first problem we face is that of the extent of effective sanctions. In the following analysis I have assumed very modestly that the effectiveness parameter = 0.5. This means that any export embargo is only 50 percent effective. Through a combination of cheating, ingenuity, and other innovative forms of behavior South

Figure 2

Format of the South African SAM (Numbers under Each Account Represent the Various Sectors Appearing in the SAM, e.g., 40 Different Factors, 28 Households)

| | | ENDOGENOUS ACCOUNTS | | | EXOGENOUS ACCOUNTS | | | | |
	Factors 1–40	Households 41–68	Companies 69	Production Activities 70–93	Government 94	Capital Account 95	Net Indirect Taxes 96	Rest of the World 97	Total
Factors 1–40				Allocation of Labor and Capital Value Added to Factors				Factor Income Received from Abroad	Total Incomes of Factors
Households 41–68	Allocation of Labor and Uninc Capital Income to Households	Current Transfers Among Households	Profits and Dividends Distributed to Households		Current Transfers to Households			Nonfactor Income Received from Abroad	Total Incomes of Households
Companies 69	Allocation of Inc Operating Surplus to Companies				Current Transfers to Domestic Companies				Total Incomes of Domestic Companies
Production Activities 70–93		Household Consumption Expenditures on Domestic Commodities		Domestic Intermediate Input Requirements	Government Current Expenditures On Domestic Commodities	Investment Expenditures on Domestic Goods		Exports	Aggregate Demand = Gross Output
Government 94		Direct Taxes	Direct Taxes on Companies				Net Indirect Taxes	Net Nonfactor Incomes Received from Abroad	Total Government Receipts
Capital 95		Household Savings	Undistributed Profits After Tax		Government Current Account Surplus			Net Capital Received from Abroad	Aggregate Savings
Net Indirect Taxes 96				Net Indirect Taxes				Net Indirect Taxes on Exports	Total Indirect Taxes
Rest of the World 97	Factor Payment Abroad	Household Consumption Expenditures on Imported Goods	Nonfactor Payment Abroad	Imports of Intermediate Inputs	Government Current Expenditures on Imports	Imports of Capital Goods			Total Foreign Exchange Expenditures
Totals	Total Expenditures of Domestic Factors of Production	Total Expenditures of Households	Total Expenditures of Companies	Total Costs of Gross Output	Total Expenditures of Government	Aggregate Investment	Total Indirect Taxes	Total Foreign Exchange Receipts	

(Rows are RECEIPTS; columns are EXPENDITURES. ENDOGENOUS ACCOUNTS and EXOGENOUS ACCOUNTS as labeled. Institutions comprise Households and Companies.)

Source: Compiled by the author from CEAS (1986).

Africa will be able to sell half the amount of its banned output. The studies by the U.S. General Accounting Office (GAO) pointed out that sanctions may have led to a loss of $400 million per annum of South African exports.[8] We divide this by 2 in order to be conservative. In the following experiments we carry this analysis further by looking at a reduction of a $20 million demand in each of the 10 major sectors of the South African economy listed in the following tables.

Table 1 gives the fixed price multipliers for all 10 sectors. Along the row are listed the 93 endogenous accounts. The impact of any fixed amount of export ban of any of the 10 commodities can be traced on the sectors listed along the rows by multiplying the sanctioned amount by the multiplier in the intersection of that particular row and column. For example, the impact of a $10 million embargo on agriculture on white professional income will be $10 $\times$ .0287 = $287,000. We now carry out our analysis by referring to our earlier "realistic" figures of $20 million embargo on each of the 10 sectors.

The output effect is shown in Table 2. I have broken it down into two columns. The first column shows the total (direct plus indirect) effects of the sanction on output. The second column gives only the direct effect. The difference between the two (which is not shown in Table 2 but can be calculated easily) gives the indirect effect.

Looking at Table 2 one can observe the large effects of even moderately effective sanctions. In agriculture the total effect is a reduction of output of $75.9 million, which is 3.75 times the embargoed amount. The value of reduced output varies but is nowhere less than 3 times the original sanctioned amount. In three sectors, food ($94.39 million), leather ($90.30 million), and wood ($92.14 million), the multiplier is 4.5 or more.

The second important observation from Table 2 is the predominance of indirect effects. These indirect effects derive from mainly two sources. First, a decrease in output in a sector initially reduces its output and hence the input it buys from other sectors, whose outputs are then reduced. There is then a further reduction of the output of the original sector and so on. This is the familiar input-output story. In SAM, however, there is a further source of reduction from the indirect effects operating through the households. A reduction of output leads to a reduction in payments to and hence incomes of households. The households then reduce their consumption of various commodities in accordance with their purchasing habits. This leads to the Keynesian multiplier effect. The SAM-based multipliers combine these two effects. The section on structural path analysis offers further insights into the study of these indirect effects.

The contraction of output will lead to a contraction of employment. The detailed impact of sanctions on employment by sectors and by

Table 1
Fixed Price Multiplier Matrix: Ten Main Sectors

Key To Abbreviations

AGRICUL	Agriculture, hunting, forestry and fishing
GOLD	Gold mining
MINING	Other mining
FOOD	Food manufacturing
BEVERAGE	Beverage manufacturing
TOBACCO	Manufacture of tobacco products
TEXTILES	Manufacture of textiles
WEARING	Manufacture of wearing apparel
LEATHER	Leather, leather products and footwear
WOOD	Wood, wood products and furniture
PAPER	Paper, paper products, printing and publishing
CHEMICAL	Chemicals, chemical products, plastics and rubber products
N_M_MINS	Non-metallic minerals and products
BAS_META	Basic metal industries
FAB_META	Fabricated metal products, machinery and transport equipment
MISC_FAB	Other manufacturing industries
ELECTR	Electricity, gas and steam
WATER	Water supply
CONSTRUC	Construction
TRADE	Commerce
TRANSPOR	Transport, storage and communication
FINANCE	Financing, insurance, real estate and business services
COM_SERV	Community, social and personal services
OTHER	Other
CAPITAL	Capital

Population Groups

W_	Whites
C_	Coloureds
A_	Indians
B_	Blacks

Occupations

_Prof	Professional
_Tech	Technical
_Opro	Other professional
_Admi	Administrative
_Cler	Clerical
_Sale	Sales
_Serv	Services
_Farm	Farm workers
_Labr	Labourers
_Nucla	Not classified elsewhere

Households

_Q1	First income quintile 0-20% of population
_Q2	Second income quintile 21-40% of population
_Q3	Third income quintile 41-60% of population
_Q4	Fourth income quintile 61-80% of population
_Q5a	Ninth income decile 81-90% of population
_Q5b	Tenth income decile 91-95% of population
_Q5c	Tenth income decile 96-100% of population

Table 1 (Continued)

		Name	Production Sectors AGRICUL 1	GOLD 2	MINING 3	FOOD 4	TEXTILES 7
P	1	AGRICUL	1.1765	0.093	0.0857	0.6192	0.1616
r	2	GOLD	0.0005	1.0006	0.0007	0.0006	0.0006
o	3	MINING	0.018	0.0198	1.0253	0.0226	0.0242
d	4	FOOD	0.1916	0.105	0.1025	1.3771	0.1125
u	5	BEVERAGE	0.0211	0.0237	0.0233	0.0244	0.0231
c	6	TOBACCO	0.0041	0.0046	0.0046	0.0047	0.0046
t	7	TEXTILES	0.0347	0.0321	0.0336	0.0429	1.4063
i	8	WEARING	0.0178	0.0205	0.0205	0.0206	0.0198
o	9	LEATHER	0.0082	0.0092	0.0091	0.0091	0.009
n	10	WOOD	0.0144	0.0121	0.0134	0.015	0.0127
	11	PAPER	0.0404	0.0305	0.0409	0.0765	0.0563
S	12	CHEMICAL	0.1964	0.113	0.1722	0.1978	0.2792
e	13	N_M_MINS	0.0087	0.0069	0.0097	0.0164	0.0075
c	14	BAS_META	0.0299	0.0353	0.0544	0.0364	0.0278
t	15	FAB_META	0.0903	0.1057	0.1777	0.1156	0.0876
o	16	MISC_FAB	0.003	0.0037	0.0042	0.0038	0.0041
r	17	ELECTR	0.0355	0.0677	0.0716	0.049	0.0557
s	18	WATER	0.0072	0.0083	0.0102	0.0094	0.01
	19	CONSTRUC	0.0059	0.0029	0.0038	0.005	0.0036
	20	TRADE	0.2649	0.2095	0.2679	0.2869	0.2598
	21	TRANSPOR	0.1203	0.1014	0.131	0.1804	0.1436
	22	FINANCE	0.14	0.134	0.1614	0.1951	0.1938
	23	COM_SERV	0.0391	0.0418	0.0465	0.0479	0.0437
	24	OTHER	0.0339	0.0534	0.1062	0.0807	0.0725
F	25	W_Prof	0.0287	0.0345	0.0375	0.0376	0.0375
a	26	W_Tech	0.0118	0.0132	0.0154	0.0157	0.0162
c	27	W_Opro	0.0027	0.0026	0.003	0.0039	0.0043
t	28	W_Admi	0.0344	0.0294	0.0406	0.0523	0.0567
o	29	W_Cler	0.0401	0.0381	0.0471	0.0576	0.054
r	30	W_Sale	0.0359	0.0284	0.0371	0.0452	0.0459
s	31	W_Serv	0.0056	0.0054	0.0062	0.0072	0.0061
	32	W_Farm	0.016	0.0017	0.0016	0.0088	0.0024
	33	W_Labr	0.0423	0.0897	0.087	0.0678	0.0679
	34	W_Nucla	0.0012	0.0015	0.0023	0.0019	0.0016
	35	C_Prof	0.0013	0.0013	0.0017	0.0016	0.0021
	36	C_Tech	0.0006	0.0004	0.0007	0.0009	0.0014
	37	C_Opro	0.0001	0.0001	0.0001	0.0001	0.0001
	38	C_Admi	0.0004	0.0004	0.0005	0.0005	0.0006
	39	C_Cler	0.0043	0.0035	0.0049	0.0062	0.0087
	40	C_Sale	0.0026	0.002	0.0026	0.0032	0.0037
	41	C_Serv	0.0027	0.0026	0.0032	0.0035	0.0046
	42	C_Farm	0.0223	0.0021	0.002	0.013	0.0034
	43	C_Labr	0.0157	0.0131	0.0208	0.0281	0.0468
	44	C_Nucla	0.0004	0.0004	0.0008	0.0007	0.0008
	45	A_Prof	0.0007	0.0007	0.0008	0.0011	0.0014
	46	A_Tech	0.0003	0.0003	0.0004	0.0005	0.0008
	47	A_Opro	0	0	0	0.0001	0.0001

Table 1 (Continued)

		Name	Production Sectors				
			WEARING 8	LEATHER 9	WOOD 10	CHEMICAL 12	N_M_MINS 13
P	1	AGRICUL		0.1639	0.1925	0.0821	0.099
r	2	GOLD		0.001	0.0008	0.0005	0.0037
o	3	MINING	0.1285	0.0242	0.0252	0.0557	0.0846
d	4	FOOD	0.001	0.2259	0.1411	0.0983	0.12
u	5	BEVERAGE	0.0206	0.028	0.0295	0.0187	0.0273
c	6	TOBACCO	0.1288	0.006	0.006	0.0036	0.0053
t	7	TEXTILES	0.0269	0.1324	0.0787	0.0371	0.0372
i	8	WEARING	0.0057	0.0249	0.0263	0.0165	0.0227
o	9	LEATHER	0.5561	1.1374	0.0117	0.0069	0.0103
n	10	WOOD	1.0644	0.026	1.2316	0.0106	0.0176
	11	PAPER	0.0195	0.0878	0.0598	0.0563	0.0686
S	12	CHEMICAL	0.0158	0.2968	0.2507	1.3216	0.1756
e	13	N_M_MINS	0.0684	0.0096	0.0194	0.0118	1.1217
c	14	BAS_META	0.2099	0.0334	0.0564	0.0321	0.0776
t	15	FAB_META	0.0079	0.1059	0.123	0.0835	0.1262
o	16	MISC_FAB	0.0264	0.0086	0.0048	0.003	0.0042
r	17	ELECTR	0.085	0.0509	0.0599	0.046	0.0894
s	18	WATER	0.0092	0.0096	0.0099	0.008	0.0104
	19	CONSTRUC	0.0496	0.0042	0.0045	0.0031	0.0041
	20	TRADE	0.009	0.3149	0.3298	0.2335	0.2924
	21	TRANSPOR	0.0038	0.1628	0.1676	0.1512	0.1727
	22	FINANCE	0.2778	0.2344	0.2568	0.1624	0.2179
	23	COM_SERV	0.1478	0.054	0.0569	0.0394	0.0506
	24	OTHER	0.229	0.0984	0.1056	0.0711	0.0733
F	25	W_Prof	0.0506	0.0426	0.04	0.0362	0.0426
a	26	W_Tech	0.0916	0.0152	0.0154	0.0175	0.0182
c	27	W_Opro	0.0391	0.006	0.0056	0.0035	0.0047
t	28	W_Admi	0.0139	0.08	0.0803	0.0516	0.0706
o	29	W_Cler	0.0096	0.0636	0.0674	0.0522	0.0674
r	30	W_Sale	0.0664	0.0608	0.0639	0.0437	0.0469
s	31	W_Serv	0.0568	0.0066	0.0077	0.0058	0.0071
	32	W_Farm	0.0601	0.0025	0.0033	0.0014	0.0019
	33	W_Labr	0.0063	0.07	0.0925	0.0671	0.1069
	34	W_Nucla	0.002	0.0018	0.0025	0.0018	0.0031
	35	C_Prof	0.0635	0.0027	0.0022	0.0015	0.002
	36	C_Tech	0.0022	0.0007	0.0008	0.001	0.0007
	37	C_Opro	0.0022	0.0009	0.0001	0.0001	0.0001
	38	C_Admi	0.001	0.0008	0.0032	0.0006	0.0007
	39	C_Cler	0.0011	0.0143	0.0118	0.0059	0.0077
	40	C_Sale	0.0015	0.0047	0.0067	0.0028	0.0035
	41	C_Serv	0.0161	0.005	0.0039	0.0029	0.004
	42	C_Farm	0.0057	0.0036	0.0043	0.0019	0.0024
	43	C_Labr	0.0072	0.1045	0.0767	0.0213	0.037
	44	C_Nucla	0.0031	0.0015	0.0018	0.0008	0.0006
	45	A_Prof	0.0914	0.0015	0.0012	0.0009	0.0009
	46	A_Tech	0.0019	0.0004	0.0004	0.0009	0.0004
	47	A_Opro	0.0015	0.0005	0.0002	0	0.0001

Table 1 (Continued)

		Name	Production Sectors AGRICUL 1	GOLD 2	MINING 3	FOOD 4	TEXTILES 7
F	48	A_Admi	0.0006	0.0005	0.0007	0.001	0.0014
a	49	A_Cler	0.0032	0.0024	0.0033	0.0052	0.0079
c	50	A_Sale	0.0033	0.0025	0.0033	0.0044	0.0037
t	51	A_Serv	0.0005	0.0004	0.0005	0.0006	0.0006
o	52	A_Farm	0.0007	0.0001	0.0001	0.0004	0.0001
r	53	A_Labr	0.0046	0.0036	0.0048	0.0085	0.0119
s	54	A_Nucla	0.0001	0.0001	0.0001	0.0001	0.0002
	55	B_Prof	0.0031	0.0043	0.0042	0.0037	0.0033
	56	B_Tech	0.0008	0.0012	0.0012	0.0011	0.001
	57	B_Opro	0.0001	0.0001	0.0002	0.0002	0.0002
	58	B_Admi	0.0002	0.0002	0.0004	0.0003	0.0006
	59	B_Cler	0.007	0.0085	0.01	0.0101	0.0114
	60	B_Sale	0.0074	0.0059	0.0075	0.0091	0.0082
	61	B_Serv	0..0186	0.0215	0.0236	0.0231	0.0218
	62	B_Farm	0.0865	0.009	0.0088	0.0475	0.0139
	63	B_Labr	0.0482	0.1748	0.1294	0.0866	0.1215
	64	B_Nucla	0.0024	0.0025	0.0042	0.0043	0.0048
	65	CAPITAL	0.8288	0.8232	0.7689	0.7186	0.5097
H	66	W_Q1	0.0199	0.0224	0.0225	0.0217	0.0183
o	67	W_Q2	0.0419	0.0479	0.0488	0.0475	0.0412
u	68	W_Q3	0.0642	0.0669	0.0691	0.0705	0.0604
s	69	W_Q4	0.0887	0.0959	0.1004	0.1014	0.0899
e	70	W_Q5a	0.0655	0.0693	0.0732	0.075	0.067
h	71	W_Q5b	0.0449	0.047	0.0499	0.0515	0.0463
o	72	W_Q5c	0.0788	0.0791	0.0847	0.089	0.0803
l	73	C_Q1	0.0045	0.001	0.0012	0.0033	0.0021
d	74	C_Q2	0.0075	0.0024	0.0031	0.0063	0.0055
s	75	C_Q3	0.0098	0.0039	0.0052	0.0092	0.0093
	76	C_Q4	0.0116	0.007	0.0095	0.0137	0.0173
	77	C_Q5a	0.0078	0.0057	0.0078	0.0104	0.0143
	78	C_Q5b	0.0052	0.004	0.0054	0.007	0.0097
	79	C_Q5c	0.0083	0.0067	0.0091	0.0114	0.0159
	80	A_Q1	0.0011	0.0008	0.0009	0.0014	0.0015
	81	A_Q2	0.0019	0.0016	0.0019	0.0027	0.0032
	82	A_Q3	0.0029	0.0025	0.0029	0.004	0.0048
	83	A_Q4	0.0045	0.0038	0.0044	0.0061	0.0073
	84	A_Q5a	0.0033	0.0028	0.0032	0.0044	0.0051
	85	A_Q5b	0.0024	0.002	0.0023	0.0031	0.0035
	86	A_Q5c	0.0043	0.0037	0.0043	0.0055	0.0062
	87	B_Q1	0.008	0.0033	0.003	0.0055	0.003
	88	B_Q2	0.0227	0.0118	0.0104	0.0166	0.0105
	89	B_Q3	0.0366	0.026	0.0227	0.0297	0.0222
	90	B_Q4	0.0494	0.054	0.0472	0.0489	0.0447
	91	B_Q5a	0.0357	0.0594	0.0492	0.0425	0.0456
	92	B_Q5b	0.0224	0.0467	0.0376	0.0297	0.0345
	93	B_Q5c	0.0354	0.0666	0.0556	0.0459	0.0515

Table 1 (Continued)

		Name	Production Sectors				
			WEARING 8	LEATHER 9	WOOD 10	CHEMICAL 12	N_M_MINS 13
F	48	A_Admi	0.001	0.0014	0.002	0.0007	0.0009
a	49	A_Cler	0.0003	0.0128	0.006	0.0041	0.0051
c	50	A_Sale	0.0024	0.0066	0.0049	0.0032	0.0036
t	51	A_Serv	0.012	0.0011	0.0007	0.0005	0.0006
o	52	A_Farm	0.0057	0.0001	0.0002	0.0001	0.0001
r	53	A_Labr	0.001	0.0473	0.0217	0.0056	0.0063
s	54	A_Nucla	0.0001	0.0005	0.0003	0.0002	0.0001
	55	B_Prof	0.0382	0.0039	0.0042	0.0032	0.004
	56	B_Tech	0.0005	0.0009	0.001	0.0013	0.0016
	57	B_Opro	0.0038	0.0002	0.0003	0.0001	0.0008
	58	B_Admi	0.0009	0.0005	0.0005	0.0005	0.0004
	59	B_Cler	0.0002	0.012	0.0148	0.01	0.0151
	60	B_Sale	0.0004	0.0112	0.0126	0.0072	0.0088
	61	B_Serv	0.0116	0.0244	0.0283	0.0199	0.0298
	62	B_Farm	0.0093	0.0143	0.0198	0.008	0.0099
	63	B_Labr	0.0232	0.1148	0.1412	0.0759	0.1539
	64	B_Nucla	0.0115	0.0051	0.0059	0.0035	0.0077
	65	CAPITAL	0.1338	0.5266	0.6023	0.4768	0.6303
H	66	W_Q1	0.005	0.0198	0.0232	0.0175	0.0242
o	67	W_Q2	0.4738	0.0455	0.0521	0.0396	0.0538
u	68	W_Q3	0.0181	0.0678	0.0761	0.0578	0.0769
s	69	W_Q4	0.0415	0.1025	0.113	0.086	0.1133
e	70	W_Q5a	0.0618	0.0774	0.0843	0.0639	0.0833
h	71	W_Q5b	0.0934	0.0541	0.0583	0.0441	0.0572
o	72	W_Q5c	0.0708	0.0961	0.102	0.0757	0.0975
l	73	C_Q1	0.0494	0.0034	0.0029	0.0011	0.0017
d	74	C_Q2	0.0872	0.0099	0.0081	0.0029	0.0044
s	75	C_Q3	0.0032	0.0175	0.0141	0.005	0.0077
	76	C_Q4	0.0092	0.0333	0.0264	0.0094	0.0144
	77	C_Q5a	0.0163	0.0276	0.022	0.0078	0.0119
	78	C_Q5b	0.0313	0.0182	0.0147	0.0055	0.0081
	79	C_Q5c	0.0261	0.0291	0.0247	0.0091	0.0134
	80	A_Q1	0.0174	0.0045	0.0023	0.0009	0.0011
	81	A_Q2	0.0279	0.0093	0.0047	0.0018	0.0022
	82	A_Q3	0.0038	0.0132	0.0068	0.0029	0.0034
	83	A_Q4	0.0078	0.0182	0.0097	0.0044	0.0052
	84	A_Q5a	0.0111	0.0114	0.0063	0.0032	0.0037
	85	A_Q5b	0.0156	0.0067	0.0041	0.0023	0.0027
	86	A_Q5c	0.0099	0.0116	0.0076	0.0041	0.0048
	87	B_Q1	0.0061	0.0031	0.0039	0.0022	0.0033
	88	B_Q2	0.0107	0.0107	0.0133	0.0075	0.012
	89	B_Q3	0.003	0.0226	0.0277	0.0159	0.0264
	90	B_Q4	0.0105	0.0456	0.0552	0.0329	0.0556
	91	B_Q5a	0.0228	0.0455	0.055	0.0326	0.0576
	92	B_Q5b	0.0469	0.0338	0.041	0.024	0.0437
	93	B_Q5c	0.0486	0.0519	0.0624	0.0373	0.0648

Table 2
Total Output Effect and Direct Effect: 20 Million Rands of Export Embargo in Each of the 10 Main Sectors (Figures in Millions)

	Total Output	Direct Effect
Agriculture	75.90	1.11
Gold	71.34	0.00
Mining	77.28	0.06
Textiles	82.18	5.45
Food	94.39	3.66
Wearing	78.84	0.80
Leather	90.30	2.24
Wood	92.14	3.56
Chemical	69.90	3.72
N M Mins	84.42	2.04

Source: Author's calculations from CEAS (1986).

racial-occupational categories is given in Tables 3 and 4. In the aggregate, agriculture will lose 21,964 jobs, which is the highest. The employment impact is minimum for chemicals (2,054 jobs lost). Blacks, whites, and coloureds all lose the most jobs in agriculture. If jobs are to be hurt as little as possible, sanctions against agriculture are not a good idea. Gold, however, is a good prospect since loss of jobs will be much less severe there (3,896 jobs lost). It is nevertheless true that sanctions will lead to loss of employment

The figures in Tables 3 and 4 are upper bound estimates or maximum job losses in two ways. First, the wages have been held fixed for these exercises. If there is any downward flexibility in the wage structure then fewer jobs would be lost. Second, in some of the skill categories, because of a labor shortage, it may not be optimal to dispense with the workers.

The imposition of sanctions has implications for labor and capital incomes and for household incomes as well. The results for an effective embargo of $20 million in the previously mentioned 10 sectors are shown in Tables 5 and 6. In qualitative terms, the conclusions to be drawn here are the same as in Khan (1988, 1989). Briefly, capital's loss is relatively higher than labor of all kinds. Within the household categories this is reflected in the higher loss of white upper-income households than that of any other kind of household. Thus,

Table 3
Employment Loss According to Race: 20 Million Rands of Export Embargo in Each of the 10 Main Sectors

Sector	Whites	Colored	Asians	Blacks	Total
Agriculture	1146	3082	216	17520	21964
Gold	476	116	50	3254	3896
Mining	576	142	64	2616	3398
Food	756	640	148	2320	3864
Textiles	690	698	222	2568	4178
Wearing	1048	1356	1258	1850	5512
Leather	1054	1324	632	2178	5188
Wood	988	990	228	3454	5660
Chemical	634	268	84	1068	2054
N M Mins	886	600	128	2734	4348

Source: Author's calculations from CEAS (1986), and *South African Statistics*.

to the extent that the ruling group is influenced by such losses there are reasons to expect increasing willingness to negotiate.

STRUCTURAL PATH ANALYSIS OF SANCTIONS

Considerably more insight into the process by which sanctions work can be derived by applying the structural path analysis to the fixed price multipliers. This technique was developed by J. Defourney and E. Thorbecke (1984) and has since been applied by Khan and Thorbecke (1988, 1989).

The structural path analysis breaks down the *global influence* given by the fixed price multipliers in any sector into a series of *direct influences* that act on each other and can also include feedback effects. It can be shown that each global influence (fixed price multipliers) is the sum of a series of total influences. The latter, in turn, are multiplicatively damped influences traveling from one part of the economy to another. As mentioned before, there can be feedback loops. These loops are captured by the path multipliers.

Table 7 shows some of these decompositions for a few sectors. In order to illustrate the idea of structural path analysis of sanctions I have chosen to present one example in diagrammatic form.

Table 4
Employment Loss According to Race and Occupational Categories: 20 Million Rands of Export Embargo in Each of the 10 Main Sectors

	Agriculture				Gold			
	W	C	A	B	W	C	A	B
Prof	150	80	10	312	68	6	4	60
Tech	62	36	4	80	26	Ø	Ø	18
Opro	14	6	Ø	10	4	Ø	Ø	Ø
Admi	180	24	10	20	58	Ø	2	Ø
Cler	210	262	50	704	74	16	12	122
Sale	188	160	52	744	56	10	12	84
Serv	30	166	8	1870	10	12	2	308
Farm	84	1364	10	8694	4	10	Ø	128
Labr	222	960	72	4844	174	62	18	2498
NCla	6	24	Ø	242	2	Ø	Ø	36
Total	1146	3082	216	17520	476	116	50	3254

	Mining				Food			
	W	C	A	B	W	C	A	B
Prof	76	12	4	58	96	18	8	46
Tech	32	6	Ø	16	40	10	4	14
Opro	6	Ø	Ø	2	10	Ø	Ø	2
Admi	92	4	4	6	134	6	6	4
Cler	96	38	16	138	146	68	36	126
Sale	76	20	16	104	114	36	30	114
Serv	12	24	2	326	18	38	4	288
Farm	4	16	Ø	122	22	144	2	592
Labr	178	16	22	1786	172	312	58	1080
NCla	4	6	Ø	58	4	8	Ø	54
Total	576	142	64	2616	756	640	148	2320

Table 4 (Continued)

	Textiles				Wearing Apparel			
	W	C	A	B	W	C	A	B
Prof	88	20	12	46	134	832	982	710
Tech	38	14	6	14	242	28	20	10
Opro	10	0	0	2	104	28	16	70
Admi	134	6	12	8	36	14	10	16
Cler	128	84	62	156	26	14	4	4
Sale	108	36	30	112	176	20	26	8
Serv	14	44	4	300	150	212	128	216
Farm	6	32	0	192	158	74	62	172
Labr	160	454	94	1672	16	94	10	430
NCla	4	8	2	66	6	40	0	214
Total	690	698	222	2568	1048	1356	1258	1850

	Leather				Wood			
	W	C	A	B	W	C	A	B
Prof	128	26	14	46	104	20	6	64
Tech	46	6	4	10	40	8	2	16
Opro	18	8	4	2	14	0	0	4
Admi	242	8	12	6	210	28	12	8
Cler	192	136	112	140	176	104	38	224
Sale	184	44	58	130	168	60	30	190
Serv	20	48	10	284	20	34	4	428
Farm	8	34	0	166	8	38	0	298
Labr	210	1000	414	1334	242	682	136	2132
NCla	6	14	4	60	6	16	0	90
Total	1054	1324	632	2178	988	990	228	3454

Table 4 (Continued)

	Chemical				N M Mins			
	W	C	A	B	W	C	A	B
Prof	82	10	4	26	102	20	6	48
Tech	40	6	4	10	44	8	4	18
Opro	8	0	0	0	12	2	0	10
Admi	116	4	4	4	170	8	6	4
Cler	118	40	22	82	162	78	36	178
Sale	98	20	18	60	112	36	26	104
Serv	14	20	2	164	16	40	4	352
Farm	4	14	0	66	4	24	0	116
Labr	150	148	30	628	256	378	46	1814
NCla	4	6	0	28	8	6	0	90
Total	634	268	84	1068	886	600	128	2734

Source: Author's calculation from CEAS (1986) and *South African Statistics*.

According to Figures 3 and 4 the paths of influence leading from the sector where sanctions are imposed to the ultimate destination of the influence can be broken down into many channels. In Figure 3 gold is sanctioned and we look at the top 5 percent of the income groups among the white households. It is notable that only four categories of productive assets owned by these households are sufficient to explain the decline in income. It is also interesting that income from capital is the main category influencing the incomes of the top 5 percent of the whites among the four paths revealed by the structural path analysis.

By contrast, in Figure 4 the effect on top black households when sanctions are imposed on agriculture is much more circuitous and works through several other sectors (food, chemical, transport, and trade). It is noteworthy also that capital plays a relatively minor role here. In policy terms this means that it is possible to affect the income of white capitalists much more readily through export sanctions than has hitherto been assumed. At the same time, to the extent that the

Table 5
Impact on Capital and Racial-Occupational Categories of Labor: 20 Million Rands of Export Embargo in Each of the 10 Main Sectors (Millions of Changes in Factor Incomes)

CATEGORY	Agriculture	Gold	Mining	Food	Textiles
Capital	16.58	16.46	15.38	14.37	10.19
Whites					
Professional	0.9	1.0	1.1	1.1	1.2
White collar	2.3	2.0	2.6	3.2	3.3
Farm worker	0.3	0.0	0.0	0.2	0.0
Laborers	0.8	1.8	1.7	1.4	1.4
NCla	0.0	0.0	0.0	0.0	0.0
Whites total	4.4	4.9	5.6	6.0	5.9
Coloureds					
Professional	0.0	0.0	0.1	0.0	0.1
White collar	0.2	0.2	0.2	0.3	0.4
Farm worker	0.4	0.0	0.0	0.3	0.1
Laborers	0.3	0.3	0.4	0.6	0.9
NCla	0.0	0.0	0.0	0.0	0.0
Coloureds total	1.0	0.5	0.7	1.2	1.4
Asians					
Professional	0.0	0.0	0.0	0.0	0.0
White collar	0.2	0.1	0.2	0.2	0.3
Farm worker	0.0	0.0	0.0	0.0	0.0
Laborers	0.1	0.1	0.1	0.2	0.2
NCla	0.0	0.0	0.0	0.0	0.0
Asians total	0.3	0.2	0.3	0.4	0.6

Table 5 (Continued)

CATEGORY	Agriculture	Gold	Mining	Food	Textiles
Blacks					
Professional	0.1	0.1	0.1	0.1	0.1
White collar	0.7	0.7	0.8	0.9	0.8
Farm worker	1.7	0.2	0.2	1.0	0.3
Laborers	1.0	3.5	2.6	1.7	2.4
NCla	0.0	0.1	0.1	0.1	0.1
Blacks total	3.5	4.6	3.8	3.7	3.7

	Wearing	Leather	Wood	Chemical	N M Mins
Capital	2.7	10.5	12.0	9.5	12.6
Whites					
Professional	3.6	1.3	1.2	1.1	1.3
White collar	2.9	4.2	4.4	3.1	3.8
Farm worker	1.2	0.1	0.1	0.0	0.0
Laborers	0.1	1.4	1.9	1.3	2.1
NCla	0.0	0.0	0.1	0.0	0.1
Whites total	7.9	7.0	7.6	5.6	7.4
Coloureds					
Professional	1.4	0.1	0.1	0.1	0.1
White collar	0.4	0.5	0.5	0.2	0.3
Farm worker	0.1	0.1	0.1	0.0	0.0
Laborers	0.1	2.1	1.5	0.4	0.7
NCla	0.1	0.0	0.0	0.0	0.0
Coloureds total	2.1	2.8	2.2	0.8	1.2

Table 5 (Continued)

	Wearing	Leather	Wood	Chemical	N M Mins
Asians					
Professional	1.9	0.0	0.0	0.0	0.0
White collar	0.3	0.4	0.3	0.2	0.2
Farm worker	0.1	0.0	0.0	0.0	0.0
Laborers	0.0	0.9	0.4	0.1	0.1
NCla	0.0	0.0	0.0	0.0	0.0
Asians total	2.3	1.4	0.7	0.3	0.4
Blacks					
Professional	0.9	0.1	0.1	0.1	0.1
White collar	0.3	1.0	1.1	0.8	1.1
Farm worker	0.2	0.3	0.4	0.2	0.2
Laborers	0.5	2.3	2.9	1.5	3.1
NCla	0.2	0.1	0.1	0.1	0.2
Blacks total	2.1	3.8	4.6	2.7	4.7

Source: Author's calculation from CEAS (1986).

effects can be kept isolated to those that work only through capital the black households will be protected correspondingly.

This exercise mainly demonstrates the usefulness of the new method introduced. For practical purposes, a sector by sector analysis along these lines will have to be carried out. Given the structure of SAM for South Africa, it is entirely possible to do so.

CONCLUSIONS AND DIRECTIONS FOR FUTURE RESEARCH

Several interesting conclusions emerge from the preceding. First of all, the value of the present framework for empirical analysis of the impact of export sanctions is demonstrated. Second, the actual estimates in the case of South Africa show that trade sanctions have

Table 6
Impact on Household Income Distribution: 20 Million Rands of Export Embargo in Each of the 10 Main Sectors (Millions of Changes in Factor Incomes)

Household Categories	Agriculture	Gold	Mining	Textiles	Food
Whites Q1	0.4	0.4	0.5	0.4	0.4
Q2	0.8	1.0	1.0	0.8	1.0
Q3	1.3	1.3	1.4	1.2	1.4
Q4	1.8	1.9	2.0	1.8	2.0
Q5a	1.3	1.4	1.5	1.3	1.5
Q5b	0.9	0.9	1.0	0.9	1.0
Q5c	1.6	1.6	1.7	1.6	1.8
Whites total	8.1	8.6	9.0	8.1	9.1
Coloureds Q1	0.1	0.0	0.0	0.0	0.1
Q2	0.1	0.0	0.1	0.1	0.1
Q3	0.2	0.1	0.1	0.2	0.2
Q4	0.2	0.1	0.2	0.3	0.3
Q5a	0.2	0.1	0.2	0.3	0.2
Q5b	0.1	0.1	0.1	0.2	0.1
Q5c	0.2	0.1	0.2	0.3	0.2
Coloureds total	1.1	0.6	0.9	1.5	1.2
Asians Q1	0.0	0.0	0.0	0.0	0.0
Q2	0.0	0.0	0.0	0.1	0.0
Q3	0.1	0.0	0.1	0.1	0.1
Q4	0.1	0.1	0.1	0.1	0.1
Q5a	0.0	0.1	0.1	0.1	0.1
Q5b	0.0	0.0	0.0	0.1	0.1
Q5c	0.0	0.1	0.1	0.1	0.1
Asians total	0.3	0.3	0.4	0.6	0.5

Table 6 (Continued)

Household Categories	Agriculture	Gold	Mining	Textiles	Food
Blacks Q1	0.2	0.1	0.1	0.1	0.1
Q2	0.5	0.2	0.2	0.2	0.3
Q3	0.7	0.5	0.5	0.4	0.6
Q4	1.0	1.0	0.9	0.9	1.0
Q5a	0.7	1.2	1.0	0.9	0.9
Q5b	0.4	0.9	0.7	0.7	0.6
Q5c	0.7	1.3	1.1	1.0	0.9
Blacks total	4.2	5.3	4.5	4.2	4.4

	Wearing	Leather	Wood	Chemical	N M Mins
Whites Q1	0.1	0.4	0.5	0.4	0.5
Q2	9.5	0.9	1.0	0.8	1.1
Q3	0.3	1.4	1.5	1.1	1.5
Q4	0.8	1.0	2.3	1.7	2.3
Q5a	1.2	1.5	1.7	1.3	1.7
Q5b	1.9	1.1	1.2	0.9	1.1
Q5c	1.4	1.9	2.0	1.5	1.9
Whites total	15.3	8.3	10.2	7.7	10.1
Coloureds Q1	1.0	0.1	0.1	0.0	0.0
Q2	1.7	0.2	0.2	0.1	0.1
Q3	0.1	0.3	0.3	0.1	0.1
Q4	0.2	0.7	0.5	0.2	0.3
Q5a	0.3	0.5	0.4	0.1	0.2
Q5b	0.6	0.4	0.3	0.1	0.1
Q5c	0.5	0.6	0.5	0.2	0.3
Coloureds total	4.5	2.8	2.3	0.8	1.2

Table 6 (Continued)

Household Categories	Agriculture	Gold	Mining	Textiles	Food
Asians Q1	0.3	0.1	0.0	0.0	0.0
Q2	0.6	0.2	0.1	0.0	0.0
Q3	0.1	0.3	0.1	0.1	0.1
Q4	0.2	0.4	0.2	0.1	0.1
Q5a	0.2	0.2	0.1	0.1	0.1
Q5b	0.3	0.1	0.1	0.0	0.1
Q5c	0.2	0.2	0.2	0.1	0.1
Asians total	1.9	1.5	0.8	0.4	0.5
Blacks Q1	0.1	0.1	0.1	0.0	0.1
Q2	0.2	0.2	0.3	0.1	0.2
Q3	0.1	0.5	0.6	0.3	0.5
Q4	0.2	0.9	1.1	0.7	1.1
Q5a	0.5	0.9	1.1	0.7	1.2
Q5b	0.9	0.7	0.8	0.5	0.9
Q5c	1.0	1.0	1.2	0.7	1.3
Blacks total	3.0	4.3	5.2	3.0	5.3

Source: Author's calculation from CEAS (1986).

not been completely ineffective. In fact, even under very conservative estimates they have had very strong effects.

If the results here are valid then capital in South Africa has much to fear from sanctions. Similarly, white labor will also find its way of life threatened by the imposition of sanctions. It should be recognized that black workers and households will also suffer, and extensive relief together with sanctions may be necessary if hardship on poor households in all racial groups, but especially on poor black households, is to be avoided.

If the framework presented in the first section of this chapter reflects accurately how sanctions can produce induced effects in the

Table 7
Structural Path Analysis: Global Influence, Direct Influence, and Total Influence for Selected Paths

1 Path Origin (i)	2 Path Destination >(j)	3 Global Influence IG(i>j)=mcij	4 Elementary Paths (i>j)p		5 Direct Influence ID(ij)p	6 Path Multiplier x Mp =	7 Total Influence IT(i>j)p	8 IT(i>j)p /IG(i>j) (in %)
Agriculture (AG)	White Labor (WL)	0.0422665	AG-	WL	0.003224	1.2265466	0.0039544	9.36
		0.0422665	Food- AG-	WL	0.0008765	1.5572434	0.0013649	3.23
		0.0422665	Chemical- AG-	WL	0.0017466	1.5944864	0.002785	6.59
		0.0422665	Fab_Met- AG-	WL	0.0013063	1.5510457	0.0020262	4.79
		0.0422665	Trade- AG-	WL	0.001167	1.5705574	0.0018328	4.34
		0.0422665	Transport- AG-	WL	0.0015521	1.4305775	0.0022204	5.25
Agriculture (AG)	Black Labr (BL)	0.0482294	AG-	BL	0.0053955	1.2453739	0.0067195	13.93
		0.0482294	Food- AG-	BL	0.0017657	1.5710809	0.0027741	5.75
		0.0482294	Chemical- AG-	BL	0.0021949	1.6166973	0.0035485	7.36
		0.0482294	Fab_Met- AG-	BL	0.0008352	1.5815226	0.0013209	2.74
		0.0482294	Trade- AG-	BL	0.0018224	1.5826235	0.0028842	5.98
		0.0482294	Transport- AG-	BL	0.0010943	1.4503717	0.0015872	3.29
Gold (GD)	White Labor (WL)	0.0897161		WL	0.0538757	1.047865	0.0564544	62.93
		0.0897161	Fab_Met- GD-	WL	0.0022878	1.3306736	0.0030443	3.39
		0.0897161	Electr- GD-	WL	0.0016895	1.3849549	0.0023399	2.61
Gold (GD)	Black Labr (BL)	0.1747558		BL	0.1379639	1.0680287	0.1473494	84.32
Gold (GD)	White Bottom 20 (WB)	0.0224366	W_Cler- GD-	WB	0.000262	1.0680085	0.0002798	1.25
		0.0224366	W_Labr- GD-	WB	0.0044961	1.0609035	0.0047699	21.26
		0.0224366	Capital- GD-	WB	0.0069254	1.1381895	0.0078824	35.13
Gold (GD)	White Middle 20 (WM)	0.0668758	W_Prof- GD-	WM	0.0011433	1.0922123	0.0012487	1.87
		0.0668758	W_Cler- GD-	WM	0.0010178	1.1000782	0.0011196	1.67
		0.0668758	W_Labr- GD-	WM	0.0101995	1.0953318	0.0111718	16.71
		0.0668758	Capital- GD-	WM	0.0193029	1.1673531	0.0225333	33.69
Gold (GD)	White Top 20 (WT)	0.0790906	W_Prof- GD-	WT	0.0035485	1.0870759	0.0038574	4.88
		0.0790906	W_Admi- GD-	WT	0.0014914	1.0838064	0.0016164	2.04
		0.0790906	W_Labr- GD-	WT	0.0046804	1.1032084	0.0051635	6.53
		0.0790906	Capital- GD-	WT	0.0247553	1.169925	0.0289619	36.62
Gold (GD)	Black Bottom 20 (BB)	0.0032682	Agricul-B_Farm- GD-	BB	0.0000564	1.1829236	0.0000667	2.04
		0.0032682	B_Serv- GD-	BB	0.0000601	1.0283243	0.0000618	1.89
		0.0032682	B_Labr- GD-	BB	0.0003035	1.0723018	0.0003256	9.96

Figure 3
Structural Path Analysis of Impact of Sanction: From Gold to White Top Income Group

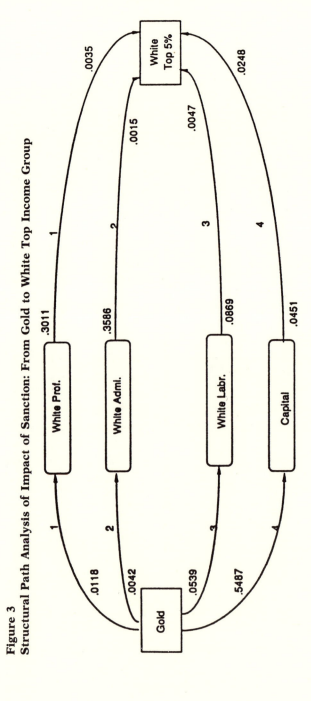

Figure 4
Structural Path Analysis of Impact of Sanction: From Agriculture to Black Top Income Group

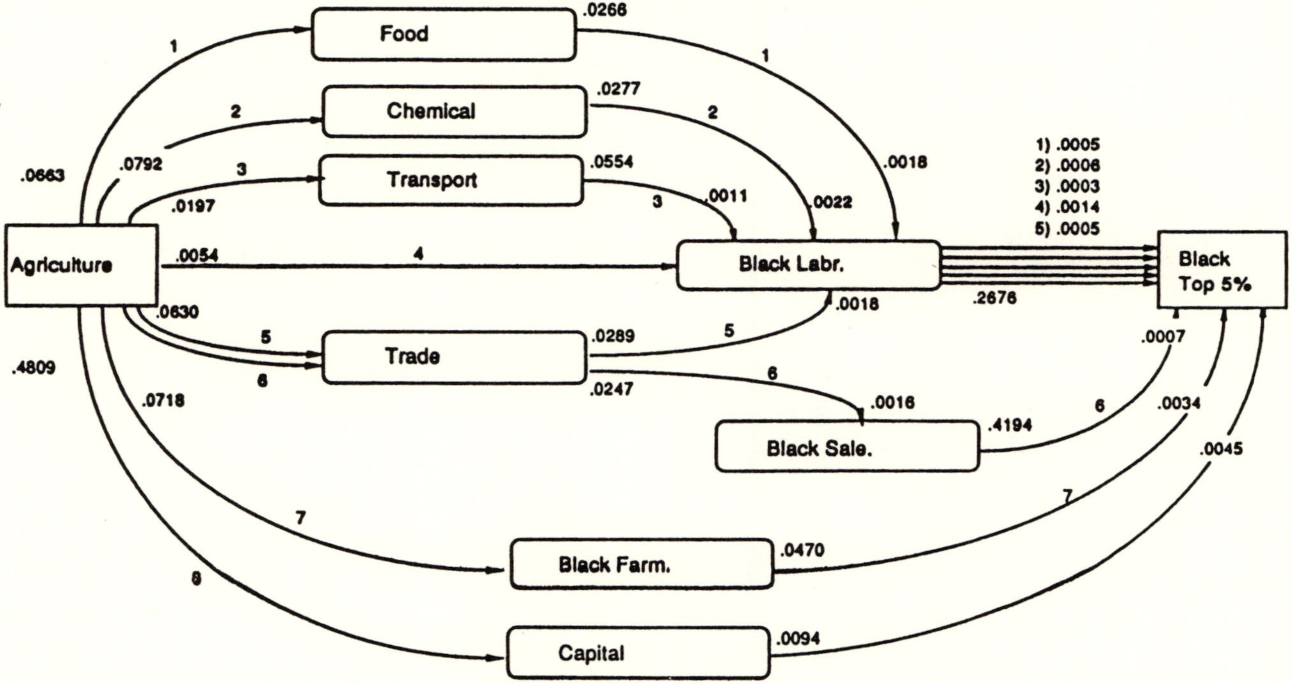

49

form of negotiations, then there are good reasons to believe that export sanctions offer some hope in this regard. As the structural path analysis shows, the effects on labor work through many more linkages than do the effects on capital. This implies that capital can be hit rather directly through such sanctions. Given that the influence of the groups thus affected is considerable in the state, even narrow self-interest should propel them to engage in some form of negotiations.

One neglected item in this analysis has been the impact of sanctions on South Africa's neighbors, e.g. South African Development Coordination Conference (SADCC) countries. It is clear that there are many economic linkages between South Africa and its neighbors through trade, employment of migrant workers, and investments. Thus any contraction of the South African economy will affect these other economies adversely. In principle, the same kind of modeling approach as has been applied to the case of South Africa could be applied to these countries. However, the main problem is the nonexistence of SAMs, or in some cases, even reliable partial SAMs. Thus work in this area requires the gathering of information for economy-wide modeling. This should be a future research task of high priority.

APPENDIX

Table A.1
South Africa's Major Exports and Imports in 1986 (Dollars in Millions)

Import

Non-electric machinery	$ 1,909
Transport equipment	1,254
Electrical machinery	1,032
Chemical elements and compounds	445
Instruments, watches, and clocks	308
Miscellaneous manufactured goods	292
Plastic materials	243
Chemical products	231
Metal manufactured goods	215
Iron and steel	181

Export

Non-ferrous metals	$ 1,697
Coal, coke, briquettes	1,405
Iron and steel	1,278
Metalliferous ores	1,041
Nonmetal mineral manufactures	733
Fruits and vegetables	621
Chemical elements and compounds	576
Crude fertilizer and minerals	322
Textile fibers	300
Sugar and preparations of honey	195

Source: United Nations data published in U.S. General Accounting Office, *South Africa: Trends in Trade, Lending, and Investment* (April 1988): 11.

Table A.2
Concentration of South Africa's Trade[a] (Figures in Percent)

Country	1982	1983	1984	1985	1986	Jan–June 1987
Import from:						
Top six trading partners	84.2	82.8	80.8	80.4	80.9	81.8
Other industrial nations[b]	13.4	14.5	16.1	16.8	16.0	14.7
Rest of the reporting nations[c]	2.4	2.7	3.1	2.9	3.0	3.5
Export to:						
Top six trading partners	84.0	83.8	83.4	83.2	81.9	81.0
Other industrial nations[b]	12.5	11.8	12.1	11.5	12.3	12.5
Rest of the reporting nations[c]	3.5	4.4	4.6	5.3	5.8	6.5

[a] A constant number of countries that reported data consistently from 1982 through the first half of 1987 was used for the table.
[b] Includes Austria, Belgium-Luxembourg, Netherlands, Norway, Sweden, Switzerland, Canada, Finland, Iceland, Ireland, Spain, Australia, and New Zealand; data from Denmark were unavailable for the second quarter of 1987.
[c] Includes Portugal, Chile, Israel, Sri Lanka, and Hong Kong.
Source: *South Africa: Trends*, 13.

Table A.3
Individual Countries' Exports to South Africa as a Percentage of Their Exports Worldwide

Country	1982	1983	1984	1985	1986	Jan–June 1987
United States	1.12	1.06	1.04	0.57	0.53	0.50
United Kingdom	2.16	1.83	1.72	1.28	1.16	1.12
France	0.67	0.52	0.52	0.38	0.32	0.30
West Germany	1.44	1.15	1.36	0.92	0.80	0.79
Italy	0.74	0.65	0.71	0.42	0.36	0.36
Japan	1.19	1.28	1.08	0.58	0.65	0.72
Hong Kong	0.78	0.70	0.66	0.31	0.34	0.45

Source: IMF, Direction of Trade Statistics, cited in *South Africa: Trends*, 15.

Table A.4
Individual Countries' Imports from South Africa as a Percentage of Their Imports from the World

Country	1982	1983	1984	1985	1986	Jan-June 1987
United States	0.80	0.78	0.76	0.60	0.64	0.32
United Kingdom	1.32	1.17	0.94	1.16	0.96	0.73
France	0.64	0.56	0.65	0.60	0.38	0.36
West Germany	0.82	0.70	0.69	0.68	0.72	0.57
Italy	1.85	1.60	2.03	2.03	1.92	1.49
Japan	1.42	1.28	1.20	1.44	1.78	1.80
Spain	0.54	0.48	0.57	0.79	0.81	0.63
Israel	1.85	1.77	1.75	1.75	1.89	1.59
Hong Kong	0.57	0.75	0.78	0.99	0.99	0.64

Source: IMF, Direction of Trade Statistics, cited in *South Africa: Trends*, 18.

NOTES

1. For a review of literature see Kahn (1989).

2. See Central Economic Advisory Service (1986).

3. Khan (1989) deals with investment and import sanctions. My ongoing work with Charles Becker attempts to model trade and investment sanctions in a unified framework.

4. For a discussion and application of this parameter see Kahn (1988).

5. See Baldwin (1985:133).

6. Spandau (1979) was the first to publish a complete input-output matrix-based analysis. Richardson (1986) followed up recently by using the same methodology. Both of them use the 1975 input-output table. Their method of open Leontief modeling also leaves the households' incomes and expenditures outside of the model. For a more detailed discussion of the contrast between the input-output and SAM approach see Khan and Thorbecke (1988).

7. See Khan (1986, 1988, 1989) for detailed description as well as technical notes in this type of modeling.

8. U.S. General Accounting Office (1988).

REFERENCES

Baldwin, David. 1985. *Economic Statecraft*. Princeton, N.J.: Princeton University Press.

Central Economic Advisory Service (CEAS), Government of the Republic of South Africa. 1986. *The Social Accounting Matrices for South Africa*. Pretoria.

Defourney, J., and E. Thorbecke. 1984. "Structural Path Analysis and Multiplier Decomposition within a Social Accounting Matrix Framework." *Economic Journal* (March): 111–136.

Khan, H. A. 1986. "Measuring and Analyzing the Economic Effect of Trade Sanctions against South Africa: A New Approach," *Africa Today* 33, no. 2:46–58.

———. 1988. "Impact of Trade Sanctions on South Africa: A Social Accounting Matrix Approach," *Contemporary Policy Issues* 6 (October): 130–140.

———. 1989. *The Political Economy of Sanctions against Apartheid*. Boulder and London: Lynne Rienner.

Khan, H. A., and E. Thorbecke. 1988. *Macroeconomic Effects and Diffusion of Technologies within a Social Accounting Matrix Framework*. Aldershot, England: Gower Publishing Co.

———. 1989. "Macroeconomic Effects of Technology Choice: Multiplier and Structural Path Analysis within a SAM Framework." *Journal of Policy Modeling* 11, no. 1 (Spring): 131–156.

Richardson, Warrior J. 1986. "The Impact of U.S. Import Sanctions against South Africa." Paper presented at the Southern Economic Association Conference, New Orleans, November.

South Africa Department of Statistics. 1980. *South African Statistics*. Pretoria.

Spandau, A. 1979. *Economic Boycott against South Africa*. Cape Town: Juta.

U.S. General Accounting Office. 1988. *Summary Report on Trade, Lending, Investment, and Strategic Minerals*. Washington, D.C.

South Africa's Strategic Mineral Exports: An Analysis of the Feasibility of a United States Embargo

_____Sanford Wright_____

The perception that the United States is dependent upon South Africa's strategic mineral exports is continually being promoted by South Africans and U.S. officials who are supportive of South Africa. In 1988, anti-sanctions efforts by the Reagan administration and legislative officials intensified. Deputy Secretary of State John C. Whitehead stated before the Senate Foreign Relations Committee that "according to the U.S. Bureau of Mines, the direct economic costs to this nation resulting from a decision to embargo South African strategic and critical minerals imports are estimated at $1.85 billion per year."[1]

Robert Wilson, the former executive director of the National Critical Materials Council, also spoke before this committee, stating: "Recently, the Bureau of Mines has estimated that a cutoff of these metals would cost the U.S. economy almost $2 billion per year, and that figure does not even take into consideration the multiplier effect."[2]

Congressman Dan Burton held a press conference on August 9, 1988, at which he stated: "Embargoing South African Rhodium supplies alone would result in 34 billion dollars in GNP losses in the second year of the embargo and 27 billion dollars in the third year even if U.S. manufacturers have adequate rhodium stocks to carry them through the first year. Furthermore, 572,000 jobs would be lost in the second year of the embargo and 458,000 other jobs in the third year."[3]

Past reports such as *U.S. Mineral Dependence on South Africa* (1982) and the *Report on South African Imports* (1987) have been utilized to promote the idea that the United States is dependent upon these imports. Nevertheless, these studies were effectively challenged by research that documented various alternatives.[4]

Several important studies published in 1988 were utilized by Congressmen Burton, John Whitehead, Robert Wilson, and other opponents of sanctions.[5] The most important study published was *Estimated Direct Economic Impacts of a U.S. Import Embargo on Strategic and Critical Minerals Produced in South Africa*.[6] Utilizing 1986 data and various economic models, this study's more important conclusions were:

1. The direct economic costs (the costs of alternate supplies) of an embargo of South African strategic minerals would be $1.85 billion per year, a total of $9.25 billion for a five-year embargo. About 94 percent of this cost reflects two platinum-group metals.

2. There are sufficient alternative sources of other minerals. These conclusions were reiterated in *South Africa: Summary Report on Trade, Lending, Investment, and Strategic Minerals*,[7] which was requested and utilized by Senators Edward Kennedy and Lowell Weicker, Jr., in preparing sanctions legislation.

Biviano et al. published an additional study, *Estimated Impacts on U.S. Gross National Product (GNP) and Employment Resulting from a U.S. Embargo on South African Platinum-Group Metal Supplies*,[8] in order to determine the potential impacts that an embargo on South African supplies of the platinum-group metals would have on automobile production, the GNP, and employment. The authors conclude that a five-year embargo on platinum and rhodium would result in GNP losses of $61 billion and over a million jobs.[9] This loss would result from decreased automobile production due to the unavailability of platinum and rhodium for use in catalytic converters.

The first study, *Estimated Direct Economic Impacts of a U.S. Import Embargo on Strategic and Critical Minerals Produced in South Africa*, contributed to the literature by substantiating that alternatives are available for the majority of South African mineral exports. However, the costs of an embargo, as presented in this report, would not only be viewed as prohibitive but also the idea of one million Americans losing their jobs would be a potent argument against applying any sanctions for fear that South Africa would implement its previous threats to withhold these minerals (counter-sanctions) in retaliation against any U.S. sanctions. Deputy Secretary of State John Whitehead reinforced this idea when he stated: "It should be pointed out that while the South African Government has never threatened the United States with a disruption or a cut-off of strategic minerals supplies, it certainly has this option."[10]

Serious questions about both of these studies exist. For example, the Soviet Union is the leading supplier of palladium, one of the two important platinum-group metals, to the Western world and the second largest supplier of platinum.

Both studies assume that Soviet-bloc sales of platinum-group metals cannot be increased, but neither study presents any justification for this assumption. In addition, neither study considered the possibility of additions to supply resulting from domestic production incentives or technological changes that affect the supply and demand of a mineral. These, and additional possibilities, will now be examined.

SUPPLY, DEMAND, AND TECHNOLOGICAL FACTORS

Supply Factors

A major assumption of both studies is that the USSR would not increase its platinum-group metal production. However, this assumption does not appear to be justified. The Soviet Union is the world's leading mineral producer and the world's major producer of platinum-group metals. The Noril'sk complex in East Siberia, which is the major site for mining platinum-group metals (PGMs), is being expanded.

Soviet platinum-group metals exports increased from 1.6 million troy ounces in 1985 to 2 million troy ounces in 1987.[11] Moreover, U.S. imports of platinum-group metals from the Soviet Union almost doubled in value in 1986, increasing from $48 million in 1985 to $81 million in 1986.[12]

The authors of the two studies may not have assumed increased Soviet sales of platinum-group metals because these metals are a co-product of nickel, and in market economy countries increased production of platinum would be somewhat dependent upon an increase in the price of nickel. However, Soviet sales to market economy countries are activated more by a desire to obtain hard currency than a response to market prices. In 1988 Soviet nickel exports appeared to be approaching another record, and the Soviets have contracted with a Finnish company to modernize their production.[13]

The large increase in prices for non-South African minerals during a U.S. embargo would certainly be an incentive for the Soviet

Union to increase its production and sales of these minerals. Perestroika (restructuring) will have an impact on every sector of the Soviet economy, and discussions are being held to increase the efficiency of Soviet mineral production and trade policy. Restructuring the Soviet economy will require vast amounts of foreign exchange. The most likely source of this will be increased exports of minerals and metals to Western countries.

Domestic Production Incentives

Neither of the two studies considered the possibility of domestic production incentives; however, legislation exists to encourage this development and potential U.S. sources have been identified. Title III of the Defense Production Act of 1950 authorizes direct federal subsidies, purchase commitments, loan guarantees, and other instruments to assure availability of essential defense materials and industrial processing capabilities.[14] These incentives could be utilized to reopen the Goodnews Bay, Alaska, site and would complement legislation passed in 1988 in Alaska that is designed to give mineral development equitable consideration with other uses of state land. The Alaskan law stipulates that a comprehensive transportation infrastructure be developed and that the state support activities that encourage mineral development.[15]

Additional Domestic Factors

Ironically, the United States presently exports rhodium and catalytic converters. The Stillwater complex produces several hundred troy ounces of rhodium, which is sold to a Belgian refiner. If present policies continue as production at the Stillwater complex is expanded, the additional rhodium will also be exported. The two studies assumed that the Stillwater production has exceeded all expectations and should double by 1990.[16]

Recycling catalytic converters is an important source of PGMs; however, possibly 65–75 percent of the recovered catalytic converters are presently being exported to Japan for extracting PGMs and recycling.

Foreign Sources Not Considered

Neither of the two studies considered the PGM reserves in Zimbabwe. The Great Dyke of Zimbabwe has many similarities with the Bushveld Complex of South Africa and contains enormous resources of important metals such as nickel, chrome, and platinum. In 1987, two companies hoped to develop the Hartley project into an operation with an annual output of 100,000 ounces of platinum and 80,000 ounces of palladium.[17]

Various studies of these deposits have been made, and Paul Jourdan has concluded:

> This resource base is clearly adequate for Zimbabwe to become a medium-sized producer, which, together with U.S. output (Stillwater) and production from the rest of the world, excluding the USSR, could replace U.S. imports from the RSA. The Zimbabwean deposits are lower grade than the South African ones and at current prices are marginal, but if a progressive embargo was imposed of, for instance, a 10% reduction of South African imports per year, as the Zimbabwean deposits were being developed, then there would be an increase in the world market prices for non-RSA or "clean" PGMs which would guarantee the profitability of the Zimbabwean operations.
>
> As the PGMs would be air freighted to the customers, any problems raised by the State Department regarding transportation through South Africa would not apply.[18]

Jourdan correctly states the contributions that Zimbabwean PGMs could make to the U.S. market; however, there would not be a need or desire to exclude USSR production or to implement a progressive embargo rather than a total embargo of South African exports.

Developing alternative sources among front-line states would enhance the effectiveness of economic sanctions by diversifying the front-line states' trade away from South Africa.

Demand Factors

The two studies shared the basic assumption that world demand would remain constant throughout the period of the embargo. However, various factors could be employed to lower demand.

The Commonwealth is currently considering various proposed sanctions against South Africa. One proposal is to end production of platinum coins and small bars as a first step toward depressing the world price.[19] If these efforts were implemented, and if Japan also eliminated its usage of platinum and rhodium in jewelry and coins, then the world price would be significantly lowered.

Technological Factors

A main source of catalytic converters will come from recycled converters, and recent technologies have resulted in a new system being marketed for recovering precious metals from scrapped converters.[20]

Converters containing rhodium have only been utilized since 1980, and as the average life of a car is about 9-10 years, they will now be coming on the market. Fifty to sixty percent of all converters could be recycled by 1995.

Research conducted at the Toyota Central Research and Development Laboratory at Aichi-gun in Japan has developed a catalyst that substitutes palladium-lanthanum for rhodium.[21] The Ford Motor Company has also developed a catalyst that does not use platinum, possibly utilizing palladium as a substitute. These developments have demonstrated that rhodium and platinum are not essential items in catalytic converters, and this technology could be expanded and utilized by other manufacturers worldwide.

An additional factor not considered was the use of alternative fuels. For example, methanol, a simple alcohol already used by race car drivers in events such as the Indianapolis 500, could be utilized as a means of reducing pollutants and simultaneously reducing the need for imported oil. Methanol has a much higher octane than gasoline and burns far more efficiently. It has been reported that Chrysler's test vehicles are putting out barely half the hydrocarbons, carbon monoxide, and nitrous oxides of equivalent gasoline-powered vehicles.[22]

ASSESSMENT OF THE ABOVE FACTORS

The two studies highly overstated the costs of a U.S. embargo of South Africa's strategic minerals. Ninety-four percent of the costs was attributable to two platinum-group metals; however, the preceding analysis presents various factors that could increase supplies, lower demand, and provide alternatives. Neither study considered the possibility of increased production in the USSR, and yet this source has been increasing its supplies since 1982 and will probably continue to do so. Neither study considered the possibility of domestic production incentives; however, the Goodnews Bay, Alaska, site could be reopened, as well as other possible sites. The studies did not anticipate that platinum production at the Stillwater site would double, and if the rhodium being mined there were not exported, and if the recovered catalytic converters that are being exported were added to domestic sources, then shortages would be greatly reduced. These possibilities, in addition to the potential Zimbabwean sources, would greatly add to U.S. and world supplies.

Demand could be lowered by simply eliminating nonessential platinum and rhodium usage in coins and jewelry.

Recycled converters could easily meet 50–60 percent of the new demand. New technology is presently assisting the recycling industry, and catalysts that substitute other metals for platinum and rhodium have already been developed.

The astronomical costs of an embargo as presented in the two reports was almost totally attributable to reductions in automobile production. At $1,200 per troy ounce, about $7.20 worth of rhodium is contained in a catalytic converter.[23] It is inconceivable that automobiles and trucks valued from $15,000 to $50,000 would not be produced due to a lack of .006 ounces of rhodium valued at $7.20. In a worst-case scenario, if for any reason rhodium were not available, then catalytic converters containing platinum and palladium could be temporarily utilized, recalling the affected automobiles for retro-fitting at a future time.

Increased supply, decreased demand, and technological advancement would result from the United States taking the lead in pressuring Europe and Japan to cooperate in these efforts. The Comprehensive Anti-Apartheid Act of 1986 required that the president take actions to ensure this cooperation, but neither President Reagan nor President Bush has done so.

Increased domestic production and a healthy recycling industry would greatly benefit the United States, and it is difficult to understand why this action has not been taken. In addition, assisting Zimbabwe in developing its mineral industry would be a step forward in developing a positive U.S. foreign policy toward Southern Africa.

CONCLUSION

This study has demonstrated that an embargo of South Africa's platinum-group metals is feasible. The high costs that have been attributed to a shortage of platinum-group metals, particularly rhodium, are not justified. Increased supplies, reduced demand, and technological advancements could place an embargo within manageable levels.

The two studies agreed that an embargo of South Africa's other strategic minerals is feasible. Therefore, a phased embargo of platinum-group metals combined with a total embargo of all other South African minerals should be immediately implemented.

The idea of South Africa withholding its mineral exports as a form of counter-sanctions is totally unrealistic. The South African economy is dependent upon these exports, and this dependency is increasing as their gold and coal exports are declining in importance and value. As Van Wyk and Von Bellow have correctly stated, "the true strength of the South African mineral wealth lies in a strategy to secure overseas markets for the strategic minerals and to strive towards increasing dependence on this region for their mineral needs."[24]

South Africa is significantly expanding its platinum-group metal production and exports in an attempt to control this market. It is difficult to understand why the United States has cooperated in this effort to its own detriment.

In light of the factors discussed above, the following recommendations are being made:

1. A phased U.S. embargo of South Africa's platinum-group metals exports combined with a total embargo of all of South Africa's other mineral exports should be immediately implemented.

2. Programs to obtain foreign sources of supply, particularly from Zimbabwe, should be immediately enacted.

3. A ban on U.S. exports of platinum-group metals and catalytic converters should be immediately enacted.

4. Domestic sources of supply of PGMs should be extensively developed, particularly the site at Goodnews Bay, Alaska.

5. The current technology utilized by Japanese firms and the Ford Motor Company that eliminates the need for rhodium and platinum in catalytaic converters should be shared and utilized in the United States.

6. Government-funded research should be immediately undertaken to develop additional alternatives to the current catalytic converter system. These efforts should be coordinated with all other countries.

7. The Strategic Mineral Stockpile should be increased to the necessary levels for an embargo, particularly of rhodium.

8. The United States should eliminate all nonessential usage of PGMs and pressure its allies to do the same.

9. The above measures should be an integral aspect of a new U.S. foreign policy that ceases all support of the apartheid regime and develops positive relationships with other Southern African countries.

NOTES

1. John C. Whitehead, "The Potential Impact of Imposing Sanctions against South Africa," *Department of State Bulletin* 88:2137 (Washington, D.C.: Department of State, August 1988), 60.

2. Robert Dale Wilson, "Statement of Robert Dale Wilson, Former Executive Director, National Critical Materials Council," *United States Policy toward South Africa Hearing* (Washington, D.C.: Committee on Foreign Relations, 1989), 155.

3. "Congressman hits Secret Japan-South Africa Rhodium Pact (Dan Burton)," *Japan Economic Newswire*, K880810004, 10 August 1988.

4. Sanford Wright, "Sanctions and South Africa: An Analysis of South Africa's Strategic Mineral Exports," in *Sanctioning Apartheid*, ed. Robert E. Edgar (Trenton, N.J.: Africa World Press, 1990); see also Joseph Hanlon and Roger Omond, *The Sanctions Handbook* (New York: Viking, 1987).

5. Marilyn Biviano, Richard Gillette, and Pamela Smith, *Estimated Direct Economic Impacts of a U.S. Import Embargo on Strategic and Critical Minerals Produced in South Africa* (Washington, D.C.: Bureau of Mines, Open File Report No. 19-88, 1988).

6. Ibid.

7. *South Africa: Summary Report on Trade, Lending, Investment, and Strategic Minerals* GAO/NSIAD-88-228, (Washington, D.C.: General Accounting Office, 1988).

8. Marilyn Biviano, Stan Miller, and George Swisko, *Estimated Impacts on U.S. Gross National Product (GNP) and Employment Resulting from a U.S. Embargo on South African Platinum-Group Metal Supplies* (Washington, D.C.: Bureau of Mines, Open File Report No. 54–88, 1988).

9. Ibid., ES-3.

10. Whitehead, "The Potential Impact," 60.

11. Richard M. Levine, *Mineral Industries of the U.S.S.R.* (Washington, D.C.: Bureau of Mines, 1988), 4.

12. Richard M. Levine, *The Mineral Industry of the U.S.S.R.* Preprint from the 1986 Bureau of Mines Minerals Yearbook (Washington, D.C.: Superintendent of Documents, 1987), 24.

13. Richard M. Levine, *Minerals Industries of the U.S.S.R.*, 6.

14. *Strategic Materials: Technologies to Reduce U.S. Vulnerability*, OTA-ITE-248 (Washington, D.C.: Office of Technology Assessment, May 1985).

15. *Mineral Commodity Summaries 1989* (Pittsburgh: Bureau of Mines Publications Office, 1989), 5.

16. Richard Doran, "Production Flows Faster than Stillwater Projections," *American Metal Market, Platinum-Group Metals Supplement* 95, no. 240 (Dec. 11, 1987): 8A.

17. J. Roger Loebenstein, *Platinum Group Metals.* Preprint from the 1987 Bureau of Mines Minerals Yearbook (Washington, D.C.: Superintendent of Documents, 1988), 11.

18. Paul Jourdan, *Independent Expert Study on the Evaluation and Impact of Sanctions against South Africa.* A study for the Commonwealth Secretariat, 1988, 13.

19. Steve Askin, "Commonwealth Weighs Tougher Anti-Apartheid Sanctions," *Christian Science Monitor*, 4 August 1989, p. 4.

20. J. Roger Loebenstein, *Platinum Group Metals*, 12.

21. Jacqui Robbins, "Autocatalysts: Converting the Public, *Materials Edge* (July/August 1988): 23.

22. Paul A. Eisenstein, "Alternative Fuels Get a New Look," *Christian Science Monitor*, 10 May 1989, p. 9.

23. Marilyn Biviano et al., *Estimated Direct Economic Impacts of a U.S. Import Embargo on Strategic and Critical Minerals Produced in South Africa*, I-21.

24. Koos Van Wyk and M. Anton Von Bellow, "The Debate on South Africa's Strategic Minerals Revisited," *Comparative Strategy* 7 (1988): 166.

4

Economic Pressure on South Africa: Does It Work?

Stephen P. Davis

Until recently, the debate over U.S. policy toward South Africa has produced surprisingly little information about the political and economic effects of tactics such as sanctions and disinvestment. In the Reagan years, Congress and the president drew battle lines along the issue of economic pressure, but too often the broader discussion over what approaches might constitute a comprehensive policy toward South Africa was lost in the fray. To act against apartheid was to favor sanctions legislation. To hinder democratic change in South Africa was to oppose sanctions. The camps were defined not so much by the wisdom or anticipated effects of economic pressure as by the dynamics of politics in Washington as the American public reacted to upheaval in South Africa. During the Bush presidency, the issue shifted to whether or not to continue sanctions in view of changes in South Africa.

This chapter attempts, first, to establish the most appropriate yardstick by which the effectiveness of sanctions and disinvestment may be measured. This involves discussing their purpose, the conditions under which they came into effect, and the obstacles they have encountered. Second, the types of economic pressures now in effect are briefly described. Third, I review whether these pressures can produce results consistent with the aims of their proponents.

PURPOSES OF ECONOMIC PRESSURE

A multitude of measures have been proposed to determine whether sanctions against apartheid "work." Opponents often suggest that sanctions need to produce tangible evidence of apartheid's demise in a short period of time in order for them to be judged effective. They cite statements such as one made by South African Communist Party chief Joe Slovo in September 1988: "I am convinced that if comprehensive and obligatory sanctions would be introduced, the ruling circles in the RSA [Republic of South Africa] would be forced to negotiate with the national liberation movement even on the most vital problems within the next six months."[1] But opponents less frequently underline the qualifiers in such predictions, namely that sanctions would have to be (in Slovo's view) "comprehensive and obligatory" in order to produce an immediate impact. Opponents reject any such action, at least as far as U.S. policy toward South Africa is concerned. But they borrow selectively from such statements in order to construct a yardstick that will inevitably measure sanctions (at any intensity) as a failure.

Ironically, many individuals who hold such views would hardly apply similar standards in measuring the efficacy of other U.S. sanctions, such as those applied against Cuba, Panama, Iran, Libya, Nicaragua, Syria, and others. In those cases, they would likely employ a more realistic gauge to evaluate sanctions. Economic pressure, for example, can be viewed as an important—but not necessarily decisive—tool for expressing opposition to a particular policy or government. It can play a symbolic role, and it can be used to raise costs the target must pay for maintaining the offending position. As William Minter has pointed out, if sanctions are judged on whether they make "a significant contribution to certain goals," then they "probably have as good a record as any alternative strategy."[2]

However, if sanctions are to play a contributing role in a foreign relations problem, they should be in an overall policy context in order to have the best chance of succeeding. They should be one important means to an end, rather than the end itself.

What is that end? In the case of South Africa, proponents of economic pressure argue that the U.S. objective should be a negotiated solution to the country's political conflict that involves all major actors, including both the National Party and the African National Congress. They contend that the primary obstacle to such an outcome is Pretoria's present unwillingness to engage in meaningful talks. This posture, they say, stems from the government's confidence that it can tough out internal and external pressures and master the pace of political change.

Confidence in unilateral control runs contrary to one of three prerequisites for talks identified by William Zartman in an analysis published in the *Washington Quarterly* in 1988. "The first condition for a negotiation is a stalemate," he suggests, "and not just a stalemate, but a mutually hurting stalemate."[3] For talks to become a live policy option, "both sides must have the impression that they cannot manage them or escalate their way out of them by themselves."[4]

Zartman and others argue that a second factor contributing to the rise of an environment conducive to negotiations is a sense of deadline, a perception on the part of the parties that problems will become "irrevocably worse" using current approaches but could improve as a result of talks.

Finally, for negotiations to proceed, there must be a "bargaining range," a situation where the parties "see each other as being willing to provide them with an acceptable outcome and must see their positions as being within reach of each other."[5]

Proponents of economic pressure believe that the United States should be focusing on enhancing the conditions for talks; that is, in effect, to take actions that promote deadlock, deadline, and bargaining range. At present, they say, such conditions are not yet in place in South Africa. The government and its constituents need to lose confidence in the omnipotence of security forces to quash resistance. At the same time, they must be galvanized into change by a sense that time is running out. In addition, they must perceive that it would be possible to preserve many of their interests in a negotiated outcome to the conflict.

Sanctions advocates suggest that a comprehensive U.S. policy taking these aims into account would include a set of sticks and carrots. Economic pressure, they believe, is a vital component not only because it can directly bring down the government, but also because it can increase Pretoria's costs in maintaining minority rule and foster a perception of harmful isolation from the outside world. Sanctions can also encourage resistance because they signal a clear condemnation of apartheid. They propose, too, that political and diplomatic pressure be linked to economic sanctions so as to strengthen the "sticks." Together, proponents believe, these effects can weaken white confidence and drive the community toward the realization that problems cannot be solved in the absence of all-party negotiations.

At the same time, they argue for incentives fashioned to help convince both sides that negotiations can produce attractive rewards and acceptable outcomes. Presently, many whites fear that the only alternative to minority rule is, in the words of the *Financial Mail*, "the surefire instant poverty of totalitarian socialism that is creating misery, on an unprecedented scale in modern times, to the north."[6] An October 1988 poll showed that 80 percent or more of urban whites believed that in the event of "black majority rule" property rights would come under challenge, communist policies would be introduced, law and order would break down, whites would suffer discrimination, crime would escalate, living standards would decline, and their way of life and culture would be threatened.[7]

Proponents point out that as long as many whites see talks leading to an Idi Amin-like future, a situation far worse than they know today, they will resist them. A comprehensive U.S. policy, however, could include measures to promote moderation in the resistance. Such actions could encompass putting ideas forward in dialogues with groups such as the African National Congress (ANC), coordinating policy with the frontline states, which support compromise, and working with the Soviet Union on ways to encourage realistic demands and thereby narrow the bargaining range.

Sanctions should be evaluated in this more realistic light, as "one of a number of different tactics that can be used simultaneously to bring down the apartheid regime," as Washington Office on Africa executive director Damu Smith told the Senate Foreign Relations Committee in June 1988.[8] But have sanctions been applied as their advocates desired?

OBSTACLES

In 1986, the Congress commandeered U.S. policy toward South Africa by enacting the Comprehensive Anti-Apartheid Act (CAAA) over President Reagan's veto. The Congress does not often or willingly engage in such wholesale assaults on a president's foreign policy. Normally, the legislature confines itself to occasional hit-and-run attacks on a specific foreign policy budget item, ambassadorial nomination, or arms agreement.

In recent decades, this type of congressional rebellion has occurred in only a handful of cases. Under Presidents Johnson and Nixon, it was the Vietnam war; under President Carter, the Salt II arms control treaty with the Soviet Union; under President Reagan, U.S. intervention in Nicaragua and policy toward South Africa. They occur, very simply, when the president's policy so significantly diverges from public opinion that large numbers of elected officials assume they will pay unacceptable political costs for endorsing it, and instead reap rich political rewards by defying it.

Ronald Reagan, rather than altering his policies enough to accommodate public sympathy with the 1985–1986 uprising in South Africa, accepted Congress' challenge. He battled the Hill until October 2, 1986, when even the Republican-controlled Senate voted overwhelmingly with the House to adopt the CAAA.

The result was in many ways unsatisfactory for both sides. Congress, for one, is institutionally ill-equipped to manage a comprehensive policy. It can usually only focus on one prominent aspect of an issue rather than a broad approach. Moreover, a legislature, by its nature, has a short attention span and cannot thoroughly monitor the executive over an extended period.

Therefore, the new made-in-Congress U.S. policy toward South Africa focused heavily on economic pressure but grappled only lightly with other aspects of Washington's relations with Pretoria. In addition, Congress' foreign policy committees could not readily sustain sufficient attention to the issue to prevent the administration from acting out what TransAfrica executive Director Randall Robinson termed its "unbridled hostility" toward sanctions by undermining the act.[9]

For its part, the executive branch found its credibility in tatters throughout southern Africa. Pretoria's rulers discovered that they could no longer rely on the Reagan administration's ability to fend off its critics. On the other hand, the antiapartheid opposition continued to accuse the White House of favoring the National Party government. The Angola/Namibia negotiations proved useful in deflecting attention from this policy incoherence, and helped to restore a sense that the United States has a future as a diplomatic "honest broker" in the region. The Bush era dawned, however, with few hints on how the administration planned to reconceptualize United States policy to account for Congress' action in 1986, since the new president had carefully avoided any commitments on southern Africa during the 1988 election campaign. Still, by mid-1989 it was clear that, in contrast with Reagan, Bush had at least accepted the legitimacy of the 1986 sanctions and was seeking a bipartisan consensus with Congress on new approaches.

Important casualties in the contest for control over United States policy toward South Africa were clarity and coherence. Rather than having economic pressure incorporated into an overall U.S. approach toward southern Africa, a strategy advocated by sanctions proponents, Washington sent mixed and contradictory messages to the region. Moreover, the Reagan administration, having failed to harmonize policy at home, made little effort to coordinate approaches with America's allies. As a result, Canada, the European Community, Britain, the Commonwealth, Japan, and other nations adopted varying sanctions and penalties on South Africa, none of which matched the CAAA in its entirety, while the West spoke in many voices on apartheid (see Appendix A).

An additional complicating factor was the way in which another economic pressure—disinvestment—materialized. United States companies began leaving South Africa in large numbers in 1985, when 40 ended their direct investments. Fifty departed in 1986, another 54 in 1987 and a further 28 in 1988. As of April 26, 1989, only 136 U.S. corporations remained in South Africa of the 325 that were reported there in 1983. By July 1989, 10 more, including two of the largest— Mobil and Goodyear—had announced plans to leave.[10] But disinvestment proceeded as a corporate trend responding to American protest and South African political and economic instability rather than to a national policy crafted to produce targeted results. Companies pulling out gave different reasons and adopted different withdrawal approaches, and many (57 out of 114 companies that have disinvested since January 1, 1986) maintained nonequity ties that diluted the impact of their departures.[11] Few disinvestment advocates either in the United States or South Africa had studied, reached consensus, or prepared guidelines on how, in their view, the process should take place.

In sum, economic pressures have evolved piecemeal, in the absence of domestic or international consensus, and without being anchored to an overall policy approach to apartheid. It should be no surprise that confusion abroad produced a measure of bewilderment, bitterness, cynicism, and defiance in South Africa's white community. The incoherence enabled Pretoria to characterize these policies as merely the actions of foreign politicians pandering to local constituencies with no understanding of South Africa. Businessmen complained of shifting goal posts. Others said that the outside world carried a stick but no carrots, that no changes would satisfy "the santioneers." Critics of economic pressure in the United States and elsewhere began to advance the conclusion that sanctions had failed.

In fact, however, what appears most surprising today is how much effect economic pressure has had in South Africa despite the policy incoherence that characterized its birth.

PRESSURES IN PLACE

The United States Comprehensive Anti-Apartheid Act of 1986, written in large part by a coalition of moderate Republicans and Democrats in the Senate, produced a smorgasbord of pressures on South Africa. The selection was the result of compromise between forces lobbying for maximum sanctions against apartheid and those concerned with protecting domestic economic interests.

The act banned certain imports into the United States from South Africa, such as gold Krugerrands, iron and steel, uranium, coal, agricultural products, textiles, and military articles. It prohibited a number of U.S. exports to South Africa, including petroleum, nuclear materials and technology, and computers for "apartheid-enforcing agencies." In addition to sanctions on trade, the CAAA imposed a variety of sanctions on capital, with perhaps a greater long-term impact. It barred virtually all new U.S. loans to South Africa and virtually all new investment in South Africa. The act also cut direct air links between the two countries.

In 1987 a new economic pressure was added when President Reagan signed a deficit reduction bill that included the administration-opposed Rangel amendment. The measure ended U.S. tax credits for income taxes paid by corporations to South Africa. Until then, companies repatriating profits from South Africa had been allowed to offset any U.S. tax obligations incurred on those profits with a credit for the South African taxes already paid on those earnings.[12] Mobil Corporation's surprise decision in April 1989 to withdraw from South Africa was prompted in large part by Rangel's burdensome tax effects, at least according to the management statement.[13] In addition to sanctions enacted at the federal level, 30 U.S. jurisdictions (as of December 1988), including cities, counties, and two states, have contracting procedures that either bar companies doing business in South Africa from winning government contracts or put such companies at a disadvantage in the bidding process. Among the cities with antiapartheid regulations are such major purchasers as Los Angeles, San Francisco, New York, and Washington, D.C.[14]

In recent years, disinvestment pressures on U.S. corporations operating in South Africa have stemmed from increasing shareholder activity as well as selective contracting penalties and federal legislation. In 1988, some 87 resolutions concerning South Africa were voted on at corporate annual meetings in the United States.[15] More than 100 were proposed for the 1989 proxy season.[16] Mobil Corporation's withdrawal from South Africa was expected to mark the start of a new round of corporate withdrawals from the republic.

These recently imposed economic pressures on South Africa are the strongest but not the first U.S. sanctions against apartheid. In 1963, the Kennedy administration imposed a voluntary embargo on the sale of arms to South Africa, as well as some restrictions on Export-Import Bank financing. In 1979, President Jimmy Carter banned Eximbank loans for the South African government and parastatals, and restricted export credits to firms not adhering to the Sullivan Principles. Carter also supported the mandatory 1977 arms embargo in the Security Council and, in 1978, banned the sale of all goods to the South African police and military.

Outside the United States, individual countries and regional organizations have endorsed widely varying economic sanctions against South Africa, which are enforced and monitored in widely varying ways. At September 1985 and September 1986 summits the European Community adopted measures including a suspension of new direct investments in South Africa, a ban on exports of arms, petroleum, and certain high-technology goods to the republic, and a ban on imports of Krugerrands, iron, and steel from South Africa.

Nordic country sanctions include an end to new investment in South Africa plus a tightening of visa requirements and termination of sporting ties and air links. The Commonwealth's officially endorsed sanctions echo those adopted elsewhere, including a ban on new investment and termination of air links. They add a prohibition on imports of South African coal, iron, steel, and uranium and withdrawal of all consular facilities in South Africa. Other important trading nations such as Japan and Israel have implemented some of the restrictions fashioned by the regional organizations.[17]

International banks imposed what came to be known as financial sanctions in 1985, when they refused to roll over loans to South Africa and then compelled Pretoria to agree to onerous repayment terms. Many such agreements are set to be renewed or renegotiated in 1990 and 1991.[18]

ECONOMIC EFFECTS

The impact of economic pressure may be assessed by examining economic data, but analysts must take into account that such measurements cannot in themselves reveal whether or not sanctions are contributing to the achievement of the intended political objectives. It is possible, for instance, that a mere threat to apply sanctions, one that in itself causes little or no economic damage, could help produce significant political movement in the desired direction. The Japanese government, for example, agreed to adopt sanctions against South Africa when it sensed the mere possibility of U.S. and European commercial measures aimed at pressuring it to do so. Alternatively, economic pressure could cause extreme economic pain but result in little or no positive political change. Panama is the most obvious and recent example.

An understanding of the way the target in all its complexity responds psychologically to pressure is necessary if one hopes to learn whether sanctions contribute to or hamper achievement of certain political objectives. One would want outlines of several important variables. Among them:

1. To what extent do target constituencies perceive that economic pressure is linked to specific political demands, or do they consider sanctions random or self-serving?

2. To what extent do target constituencies view the demands accompanying sanctions as offering a future better or worse than current or anticipated conditions?

3. To what extent do target constituencies perceive economic pressure as a one-time shot or an ongoing assault that will escalate in intensity?

4. To what extent are target constituencies confident of their country's ability to skirt or outlast sanctions in the short and long terms?

5. How high a price are target constituencies willing to pay, and for how long, to maintain policies that sanctioning powers find objectionable?

Data developed by the Investor Responsibility Research Center (IRRC) through an innovative survey that included focus groups and a public opinion poll conducted among whites in South Africa in 1989, produced some answers to these questions. One finding is that a large number of whites believe the country to be vulnerable to outside economic pressures, and might be inclined to endorse considerable change to get them lifted—except that they are extremely uncertain about what is being asked of them, and whether undertaking such actions would indeed result in an end to sanctions. The motives and intentions of foreign governments are likely to be perceived as both suspect and unclear. In the meantime, it is at least possible to review briefly some of the economic impacts of sanctions as they have been applied so far, and to infer from the course of South African politics whether they have helped or hindered movement toward positive political change.

Disinvestment

The withdrawal of foreign companies from South Africa has produced mixed results. At the micro level, it is clear that some white South African firms have benefited; almost three-fifths of disinvestments have occurred by means of sales to local white investors. Similarly, departing companies pursue "objectives which usually have very little in common with those of the activists pushing for disinvestment.[19] As a result, antiapartheid messages or plans that might attend such withdrawals may get lost in the confusion.

The biggest withdrawal—that of Mobil Oil—is a case in point. The Chemical Workers Union sued to delay Mobil Corporation's disinvestment until management negotiated with it on the ways to secure black worker protections in the new company. Gencor, the conglomerate that purchased Mobil's operations, is known as a particularly harsh employer.

Another downside of disinvestment is that the maintenance of non-equity ties has convinced many South Africans that disinvestment is a cynical sham. They may still obtain many products and services that were available before withdrawals, though in some cases names are changed.

At the macro level, however, disinvestment has a significant impact because it starves South Africa of capital and technology, and because it bolsters a sense of harmful isolation. It undermines the notion that "business as usual" is possible in South Africa without major political change. Disinvestment has "contributed to an overall atmosphere of uncertainty which has been damaging to the confidence required for earnings and investment to flourish," concludes a 1988 Commonwealth study.[20]

Financial Sanctions

The combination of the "bankers' sanctions" and national prohibitions on new investment in South Africa has severely constrained the republic's ability to gain access to capital. The Commonwealth report found financial sanctions to be the most effective measure "in restricting economic growth through forcing large capital account deficits to repay maturing loans and requiring corresponding current account surpluses."[21] In other words, Pretoria must run large balance of payments surpluses to meet its international debt and interest payments.

That, in turn, forces it to restrict imports—in effect, to self-impose certain trade sanctions—with tariffs that have become increasingly onerous as export markets suffer from world trade sanctions on South Africa and a slumping gold price. Yet, since South Africa's economic welfare has long relied on inputs of external capital and goods, import restrictions themselves constitute a severe brake on growth. Disinvestment and foreign prohibitions on new investment in the republic exacerbate the situation.

The result is an apparent ceiling on growth. Many economists argue that South Africa needs an annual growth rate of approximately 5 percent to absorb new job-seekers entering the market each year. It would need even more rapid growth to reduce the already enormous number of unemployed workers (an estimated 25–35 percent, most of whom are black). But Pretoria believes international financial sanctions compel it to cap growth at approximately 2.5 percent to 3 percent each year, a policy that generates economic insecurity, a steady decline in living standards, and a continuing outflow of capital. The *Financial Mail* labeled the process "our progressive impoverishment."[22]

Trade Sanctions

Under the impact of economic pressure, the South African rand has lost more than half it value since 1982, making the country's exports cheaper and imports more expensive. As a consequence, the republic has reported trade surpluses since 1985. Yet a U.S. General Accounting Office report issued in 1988 estimated that American sanctions "cut South African exports by $417 million" and that Pretoria "not only was unable to recover these losses by redirecting trade to other countries but also lost additional trade in these markets, resulting in a total trade reduction in goods under sanction of $469 million."[23] A 1989 study by Joseph Hanlon, which was commissioned by the Commonwealth, estimated that sanctions had cost South Africa a 7 percent drop in foreign trade.[24]

One cannot be confident of obtaining exact measurements of the impact of trade sanctions, as the South African government has classified much of the data. In addition, trade figures do not reflect the large costs Pretoria has shouldered in efforts to foster otherwise uneconomical domestic substitutes for imports. In response to the oil embargo, for instance, the government poured an estimated $11 billion into Sasol oil-from-coal plants, nuclear power, a strategic reserve, and various other capital-intensive energy projects between 1973 and 1984. In response to the arms boycott, Pretoria devoted huge new resources to develop Armscor. South African consumers have had to pay significant premiums and taxpayers significant increases to finance counter-sanctions measures. As far as the effect on employment is concerned, it appears that jobs have been lost in export-related industries as a result of sanctions, but they have expanded in sectors devoted to import substitution.[25]

The accretion of costs, premiums, lost investments, and technological isolation associated with external economic pressure has been slow but steady. The South African economy in some ways appeared to perform better than expected in 1988 (growth registered at 3.2 percent), but government figures are viewed as increasingly unreliable. Inflation, for example, was measured in late 1988 at 26 percent by some economists, while Pretoria pegged it officially at just 13 percent. The outlook for 1989 and beyond is grimmer, especially if the gold price remains low or declines further. A TrustBank forecast prepared for Assocom, the Association of Chambers of Commerce and Industry, suggested in October 1988 that "the real pain of international economic isolation will only be felt in 1989 and later" owing to the stunting effects of sanctions and disinvestment.[26]

POLITICAL EFFECTS

Opponents of economic pressure have long argued that white South Africans would react to external sanctions by "retreating into the laager," by moving to the right in defiance. While important sectors in white politics have indeed moved to support the Conservative Party (CP) in the last two years, there is as yet no convincing evidence that this trend has occurred largely on account of sanctions. In fact, IRRC survey data suggest that those moving right tend to be working-class Afrikaners for whom sanctions are a secondary concern. Some analysts believe that these constituents have deserted the National Party (NP) for the CP because the government has projected an image of uncertainty and vacillation over the country's future. Some voters may be casting their lot with the CP out of sheer frustration at the NP's lack of vision and direction, rather than because of sanctions.

Now that we are in the third year of stiff U.S. sanctions, has South Africa retreated into the laager? By almost any measure, the answer is "no." There is some evidence of whites turning against F. W. de Klerk in by-elections. Most indicators, however, show that the white community is more bitterly fragmented and confused than at any time in recent history.

Draft evasion, often an accurate gauge of public opinion, is believed to be extremely high. In 1985, between 25 and 40 percent of whites conscripted for national service did not report for duty.[27] The government has refused since then to release statistics on the subject, though Pretoria did recently concede that nearly 15 percent of men called up for Citizen Force and Commando service in 1988 failed to show up at camps.[28] By contrast, in the Vietnam era only between 1 and 2 percent of U.S. draftees actually refused to report. In Israel, draft evasion is approximately one tenth of one percent.

Morale in the armed forces, which in conscripted armies such as the South African Defense Force (SADF) can be viewed as another indicator of general public opinion, is said to be extremely low. In 1988, some 344 members of the Defense Force attempted suicide—more than three times the number that tried to kill themselves in 1985.[29]

Polls demonstrate broad-scale white pessimism concerning the country's future, and recent group interviews conducted by IRRC suggest widespread fear among whites concerning the security situation. But rather than rallying behind the government, the Afrikaner community is in the throes of "broedertwis"—bitter fraternal conflict—across a variety of fronts. The Dutch Reformed Church has split over the moral justification for apartheid; the Broederbund, Afrikanerdom's venerable secret society, has fractured over questions of national strategy. The Conservative Party has made historic inroads into the National Party's constituency, while expanding far-right organizations have grown disenchanted not only with government, but also with each other. The National Party itself is deeply divided on political strategy, with some advocating speedier reforms and others pressing to slow them down. Reactions to Nelson Mandela's release exemplified this internal tug-of-war.

Sanctions have by no means served as the major factor in provoking such fracturing. External pressure has played some role in these developments, but a more important element has been the white community's reaction to the 1984–1986 uprising and its aftermath. But neither have sanctions served as a catalyst for unity and defiance. In fact, many observers have detected in the release of Mandela and Namibia's independence an acceleration of momentum toward new political directions. The country's political future remains uncertain; but it seems that a retreat to the laager is less likely in the foreseeable future than are accelerated negotiations with the ANC and other representative groups.   •

We are left with two important facts. First, sanctions, applied inconsistently and incoherently, have had a serious but not yet crippling economic impact on South Africa. Second, white politics in South Africa seem to be moving, inconsistently and incoherently, in positive directions. But is there a link between the two? If there is, have sanctions retarded or speeded change?

There is at present little solid data by which to come to any firm conclusions one way or another on this question. But one can at least examine the constituency most directly affected by sanctions—the white business and financial sector—for signs of linkage.

Businessmen have reacted to sanctions with anger. "The United States of America has effectively destroyed its ability to influence South African affairs," declared Christiaan van Wyk, managing director of The Trust Bank of Africa, in a widely quoted 1988 speech. "Sanctions and disinvestment, if anything, have hardened attitudes toward reform and have moreover bedeviled the economic and social requirements for reform."[30] Yet, in the same address, van Wyk appears to react to economic pressure in the way sanctions proponents have hoped.

South Africa simply cannot accept the prospect of a long-term real growth rate of only 2.5 percent per annum. . . . Such a development would be a handmaiden to abject poverty, rising social violence, increasing political instability and inevitable economic ruin. . . . The tide of growing isolation must be turned in the interest of all South Africans. An important step in this direction will be the achievement of a legitimate consensus between white and black leaders. A dramatic breakthrough is required in this respect.[31]

Similarly, Henri de Villiers, chairman of the Standard Bank Investment Corp., said that "In this day and age there is no such thing as economic self-sufficiency. . . . South Africa needs the world. It needs markets. It needs skills. It needs technology and above all it needs capital. . . . It is imperative that we do not adopt poses of defiance and bluster."[32] De Villiers added that the business community had "a special responsibility to press continually for accelerated political change."[33]

Apart from lobbying the government, other business executives moved in 1988 to find common ground with trade union and antiapartheid organizations. They helped establish the Consultative Business Movement in the wake of an internal "summit" in Broederstroom.[34]

Yet in the past two years there have been few bold efforts on a par with the 1985 meeting between businessmen and ANC leaders to challenge government policy on negotiations with the antiapartheid resistance. Indeed, many business leaders disparage sanctions and contend that South Africa can manage well despite them. "Now that the sanctions card has been played, the statistics show that apart from the coal industry where 10,000 blacks had to be retrenched, they have not had much of an influence," asserted Frederick J. DuPlessis, chairman of Sanlam. "Sanctions have been tested, and they are not working."[35]

Others argue that sanctions "work," in the sense that they cause economic damage, but that this effect undermines the strength of antiapartheid forces such as black unions and white liberal businessmen. They argue that if the outside world had offered new investment and programs to "empower" democratic organizations instead of economic pressure, South Africa would by now have made further progress toward a political solution.

Evidence supporting the political efficacy of sanctions came in May 1989 from unexpected quarters: the governor of South Africa's central bank, and several Afrikaans-language media outlets. "The economy cannot recover without political reform," declared the Reserve Bank's Gerhard de Kock, who emphasized the country's dependence on an inflow of capital.[36]

Government-controlled radio took up the call in a commentary that stated that it was "necessary for the South African economy to retain and expand its external links." The editorial continued: "These realities make nonsense of the theory that the answer to South Africa's political and economic problems is to put up the shutters and isolate South Africa from the outside world."[37]

A *Beeld* editorial was even more explicit. "Our economy cannot survive in this sort of isolation. Foreign investment and money are necessary to develop our economy, but for as long as South Africa is ideologically rejected by the outside world, the money supply will remain dry." Therefore, the pro-Nationalist newspaper concluded, "the country finds itself in a position where simultaneous political and economic reform has to be advanced."[38] These reactions to sanctions strongly back the argument that external pressures have, overall, helped to strengthen support for political change rather than further empower conservative forces.

It seems clear that sanctions have succeeded in ratcheting up the pressure on South Africa, and this in turn has helped persuade important elements in the white community to oppose government policy more strongly and effectively. But the way economic pressures have been applied has helped foster confusion about their purpose and intent, which in turn has undermined chances that the political ends of economic pressure can be achieved.

They have met some of the optimistic hopes of sanctions proponents, namely that economic pressure would produce sufficient turmoil to bring Pretoria rapidly to the negotiating table. On the other hand they have fulfilled some of the worst fears of opponents, that they would become a rallying point for pro-apartheid defiance. It may yet be too early to fully assess their real impact, since some of the effects of sanctions are only now being felt. It is possible to conclude at this stage that imperfectly applied sanctions have produced imperfect results, but that the overall trend of South African white politics offers signs of hope. What part sanctions have played in this movement as compared to, say, the influence of internal public protest or insurgency must await further research.

NOTES

1. *Rabotnichesko Delo* (Sofia), Sept. 5, 1988, Cited in FBIS, Sept. 8, 1988.
2. William Minter, "South Africa: Straight Talk on Sanctions," *Foreign Policy* (Winter 1986–87).
3. I. William Zartman, "Negotiations on South Africa," *Washington Quarterly* (Autumn 1988): 141.
4. Ibid., 142.
5. Ibid., 143.
6. *Financial Mail*, July 1, 1988.
7. *Financial Mail*, Oct. 7, 1988.
8. Testimony of Damu Smith before the U.S. Senate Foreign Relations Committee, June 23, 1988.
9. Testimony of Randall Robinson before the U.S. Senate Foreign Relations Committee, June 23, 1988. See also *Implementation of the Comprehensive*

Anti-Apartheid Act of 1986 (Washington, D.C.: Lawyers Committee for Civil Rights under Law, June 1988).

10. IRRC figures.

11. David Hauck and Jennifer Kibbe, *Leaving South Africa: The Impact of U.S. Corporate Disinvestment* (Washington, D.C.: IRRC, July 1989).

12. *South Africa Reporter* (IRRC) (March 1988): 17.

13. "Mobil News Release," April 28, 1989.

14. *Divestment Action Roundup* (IRRC), November 1988.

15. *How Institutions Voted on Social Responsibility: Shareholder Resolutions in the 1988 Proxy Season* (Washington, D.C.: IRRC, September 1988).

16. *News for Investors* (IRRC), February 1989.

17. *International Business in South Africa 1988* (Washington, D.C.: IRRC, 1988).

18. *ICABA* Newsletter No. 6, 1988.

19. Hauck and Kibbe, *Leaving South Africa*, 33.

20. *South Africa's Relationship with the International Financial System* (Toronto: Commonwealth Secretariat, August 1988), 55. See also Keith Ovenden and Tony Cole, *Apartheid and International Finance* (Ringwood, Victoria: Penguin Australia Books, 1989), 146–162

21. Ibid., ix.

22. *Financial Mail*, September 2, 1988.

23. *South Africa: Summary of Report on Trade, Lending, Investment and Strategic Minerals* (Washington, D.C.: General Accounting Office, September 1988), 3.

24. *Financial Times*, August 9, 1989.

25. See, for example, the case of Joy Manufacturing in *Financial Mail*, March 10, 1989.

26. *Finansies & Tegniek*, October 21, 1988. Cited in FBIS, December 27, 1988, p. 18.

27. Stephen P. Davis, *Apartheid's Rebels: Inside South Africa's Hidden War* (New Haven: Yale University Press, 1987), 186.

28. *Weekly Mail*, April 21–27, 1989.

29. *Weekly Mail*, April 21–27, 1989.

30. *South Africa Foundation Review*, July 1988.

31. Ibid.

32. *Wall Street Journal*, July 26, 1988.

33. *Star*, July 20, 1988.

34. *Weekly Mail*, August 12–18, 1988. See also *The Broederstroom Encounter* (Johannesburg: Consultative Business Movement, 1989).

35. *New York Times*, November 13, 1988.

36. *Beeld*, May 11, 1989.

37. Johannesburg Domestic Service in English 0500 GMT, May 10, 1989, as listed in FBIS, May 10, 1989.

38. *Beeld*, May 11, 1989.

5

The Antiapartheid Movement and International Sanctions

_____George W. Shepherd, Jr._____

In the debate over sanctions, the antiapartheid movement has been more often right than wrong. This chapter demonstrates how external pressures have come together to help produce the direction of change in South Africa. With the recognition of the African National Congress (ANC) and the ending of emergency regulations, external pressures have in turn led to the beginning of serious negotiations for settlements.

Government policy follows rather than precedes major changes in the political economy on "critical social issues" such as slavery or apartheid.[1] An entrenched group may use the power of the nation-state to retard change by these movements; but in the end injustice has increasingly given way to humanizing democratic forces. The abolitionist movement in the nineteenth century combined with economic changes to effectively eliminate slavery as a major form of labor in the world. And in the second half of the twentieth century a worldwide movement to eliminate racial discrimination and particularly apartheid has emerged.[2] This movement has taken many forms in different parts of the world. In the democratic uprisings in Eastern Europe, Latin America, and Asia, it has been part of the overall expanded recognition of human rights.

The elimination of racial discrimination has moved forward through attitude changes to public policy protection of minorities and indigenous peoples. And women have become a major subject in the struggle for racial and gender equality.[3] South Africa's apartheid has moved to the forefront because, at the end of the twentieth century, it alone retains sanction of racial discrimination.

THE SOUTH AFRICAN MOVEMENT

The antiapartheid movement and the sanctions campaign should not be regarded as external to South Africa, and therefore impacting South Africa only through governmental policies from abroad. It is a movement in which South Africans of all races have been involved from the beginning. Some have gone into exile to organize the movement. Others have remained in South Africa and paid the price of imprisonment, torture, banning, and death for their convictions.

Started in South Africa by Mahatma Gandhi and Albert Lithuli, Nelson Mandela, Trevor Huddleston, Alan Paton, and Abdul Minty, it was taken up outside of South Africa by political and intellectual leaders like George Houser, Frantz Fanon, Ronald Segal, Oliver Tambo, Dag Hammerskjöld, Julius Nyerere, and Albert Camus, to name only a few of the long list who have contributed to the external growth of this critical social movement.[4]

There have been differences over strategy. However, like the abolitionists before them, they have agreed upon one major objective: equality. Governments must abolish discrimination and create equality of citizenship.

This principle has become an established international norm of human rights in which all governments in the world are expected to cooperate.[5] While there are obvious differences of practice, it has become widely accepted in official circles that the doctrine of apartheid is intolerable. Therefore, as Ved Nanda has shown in Chapter 1, nation-states have increasingly assumed the responsibility of exerting external pressure. Sanctions became more than a major tactic, they became a goal supported by both liberals and revolutionaries.[6] As a nonviolent instrument of change it appealed especially to the Western-based "critical social movement" that sought change primarily through "peaceful means."[7]

Armed struggle has been the major strategy of the exiled Africans of the ANC and the Pan-Africanist Congress (PAC), supported by a few white South Africans, the Soviet Union, and the Non-Aligned Movement (NAM). But the armed struggle advocates also supported sanctions as a supplementary strategy, and many regarded both as indispensable.

The spread of the sanctions movement over the years has been a major barometer of the strength and support of the antiapartheid movement. Its growth has been directly related to the increase of repression in South Africa. One of the early advocates of economic disinvestment from South Africa was Byers Naude, whose religious convictions transformed him from a Broederbund leader to an anti-apartheid activist and head of the Christian Institute. The Christian Institute in South Africa stated in 1976 why it opposed further investment in South Africa: "The argument that economic growth can produce fundamental change has proven false. Many Black organizations have opposed foreign investment in South Africa, and this would be the opinion of the majority of South African Blacks if their voices could be heard."[8] The increase of the police massacres (1960), the massive military arrests in Soweto (1976), bannings and political disappearances, and the daily inequities of the separation of the races reflected the direction of policy. The series of emergency measures imposing a total police-military state on the black population in the 1980s brought into existence an open sanctions movement within South Africa that has found support among governments as well as major Nongovernmental Organizations (NGOs) in the world. It was illegal to advocate sanctions in South Africa. In 1981 and in 1988, Bishop Tutu's passport was lifted because of his advocacy abroad of sanctions.[9] Exiled leaders were less restrained. At a U.N. conference in Paris on the apartheid system, Oliver Tambo, president of the ANC, said: "As far as sanctions are concerned, there is a point beyond which Botha will not want to continue with the apartheid system."[10]

While the effects of this movement are debatable, the reality of its historical emergence and current scope cannot be denied. Moreover, it has become the symbol of the solidarity of the world's people with the suffering South Africans of all races who aspire for freedom.[11] Perhaps most important, antiapartheid has become a primary force[12] compelling the National Party to accept equality of the races and begin serious negotiations with the real representatives of the majority population—the ANC.

MILITARY BANS TO ECONOMIC SANCTIONS

The scope and growth of these international measures against apartheid have been presented in several studies. The most recent useful directory has been Elna Schoeman's *South African Sanctions Directory* (1946–1988, published in South Africa by the South African Institute for International Affairs). A few variations in this movement are worth noting: The first phase, from 1946 to 1960, was essentially a popular-based demand for action, largely based on civil rights and church movements and actively supported at the international level by the new Third World governments such as India and Ghana.[13]

A conference in London convened in 1962 under the auspices of the new governments, the ANC, and antiapartheid groups such as the Africa Bureau and the Congress of Peoples, inaugurated the first fully developed scheme of sanctions.[14] Few governments were prepared to take any steps until the reaction to the Sharpeville massacre of 1960 led in 1963 to the UN Security Council's ban on the sale of weapons to South Africa. During the 1960s and 1970s the antiapartheid movement, in conjunction with the ANC, intensified the call for comprehensive economic sanctions as well as the enforcement of military sanctions, which were widely ignored.[15] And in this period the disinvestment campaign, which sought to pressure banks and corporations to remove their economic underwriting of apartheid from South Africa, got underway.[16] This campaign, which began in the United States, soon spread to Europe and around the world.[17] The only significant official response was the adoption by the United Nations of a compulsory arms ban on South Africa in November 1977, supported by Western powers, though only seriously enforced by smaller states.[18] (Some arms continued to flow from Eastern Europe and Third World countries, with Israel and Taiwan as major third-party agents.)[19] The repression of student revolts and South African attacks on neighboring states led to increased calls for action at the United Nations. These were repeatedly blocked by Western powers, especially the United States and the UK.[20] However, Scandinavian states, together with small Commonwealth powers, began to break ranks and support the movement for economic sanctions.[21]

The first Reagan administration, under the slogan of "constructive engagement," marked the high tide of Western resistance to the sanctions movement. However, the lack of significant reform and the rising resistance of Africans in South Africa, who were brutally repressed after 1982 in a series of emergency measures under the International Security Act of 1982, gave the critical social movement the emotional base it needed.[22] Economic sanctions became an official policy of the Western world in 1986, albeit limited and unenforced. In October 1986 these sanctions were imposed upon the Reagan administration by a Congress that had begun to accept the importance of human rights considerations with the security and anticommunist considerations that had dominated foreign policy up to that time.[23] The Commonwealth adopted weaker but similar sanctions,[24] as did the European Community.[25] The Soviet bloc and Third World countries welcomed this development and for the first time the basis for a growing set of economic and military sanctions existed. The scope of these sanctions was limited, but sobering to the Nationalist Party government. As the Cold War weakened, after 1987 new conditions arose for a concerted international sanctions campaign with real teeth that began seriously to undermine the growth of the economy of South Africa.[26] This prospect constituted a new trend for Western powers under the Bush administration, which in 1989 officially accepted sanctions.[27]

Privately, the South African government viewed with increasing alarm this consolidation of forces against it. Publicly, they continued their bravado statements during the P.W. Botha government, such as that by Foreign Minister Pik Botha: "The sooner sanctions come, the better. We will show the world that we have not been made soft."[28] As skilled public relations technicians, the South African nationalists perceived, from the beginning, the potential impact on their political economic system of a concerted international campaign. They therefore illegalized its advocacy at home and attempted to counter its growth abroad through extensive and expensive propaganda campaigns.

IMPACT ON THE POLITICAL ECONOMY OF SOUTH AFRICA

The impact of a critical social movement needs to be assessed in terms of criteria that differ from the usual economic debates over unemployment, capital flight, and the rising costs of production and self-sufficiency. As Walker observed, these criteria concern such matters as political grassroots consciousness, new political action space, the growth of alternative conditions, the splintering of the dominant consensus,[29] and the takeover of the majority by the new movement despite the repression. In fact, the fiercer the repression by the state the more the movement finds support from previous passive or even opposition groups.

The growth of political consciousness within South Africa among the African and minority groups is a phenomenon that has been widely noted.[30] The origins of this new political consciousness are much debated, ranging from those who see it as a class phenomenon responding to the new industrialization and urbanization[31] to those who argue in favor of a new black pride thesis.[32] While obviously a combination of the class and political aspirations of indigenous groups, the international solidarity dimension of this new consciousness is extremely important. This is a form of repressed nationalism that sees the independence of the rest of Africa denied to them. The progress of black people elsewhere in the world, such as in the United States through the civil rights movement, the trade unions, and other major organizations of self-rule such as black churches, are phenomena greatly admired by the suppressed black majority.[33] The South African media now shows the enormous discrepancies between the affluence of the white West and the poverty the Africans see all around them.

The aspiration to freedom is not an easily measurable force in an authoritarian society, and much debate took place over who best represented African opinion. But it was seen most directly in the startling polls of black opinion about political leaders and movements.[34] Nelson Mandela and the ANC have emerged in all of this as a dominant force, despite the illegalization of the ANC and the imprisonment of its leadership. Intensive persecution of all of those thought to be associated or even sympathetic to the ANC only intensified general black support. Divisions among Africans are well documented and are frequently intense regarding leaders and tactics.[35] But Nelson Mandela became, even while in prison, the unifying political leader.

Mandela went to prison defiantly stating his principled opposition to apartheid. And in 1990, after 27 years, he emerged without compromising those views, winning him support among radicals and moderates of all races. Conservatives, including some blacks, bitterly oppose him. But the middle ground he represents among the several races is the basis of his strength. He is the most respected African leader among whites despite his insistence that violent resistance to white repression is justified if the state continues to use illegitimate force against Africans and fails to dismantle apartheid.[36]

SANCTIONS AND THE DEMOCRATIC MOVEMENT

The relationship of the new political consciousness to sanctions is based on the importance of intervention in preserving the integrity and identity of the opposition. A program of solidarity across national boundaries has protected some leaders from arbitrary arrest or "disappearances." Sanctions have given hope to people who have gained very few concessions in the domestic struggle. As a concrete manifestation of the determination of the outside world to intervene on their behalf, sanctions are a life raft in the storm. While this aid has often fallen far short of their hopes, Africans see the refusal to sell arms and computers that can be used for internal repression, the denial of oil for energy, and the closing of markets for coal and steel as giving their objectives force and the recognition they cannot get at home. This is why Bishop Tutu has referred to them as "the last nonviolent option."[37]

The struggle over new political space in South Africa has been carried out by indigenous self-help organizations that have proliferated in the past decade from civic groups to trade unions and organizations for political action, community survival, housing, credit, and self-rule. These groups, like trade unions and the United Democratic Front (UDF), have created new political space to struggle against the dominant economic and political system. Their existence has been facilitated by the external support they have received. International financial assistance and pressure has enabled them to continue. Some foreign corporations, under the disinvestment campaigns, have favored the recognition of trade union bargaining and promotion of blacks.[38] The basis of many of the community groups that form the UDF is the South African Council of Churches, which has in turn been sustained by the ecumenical community of faith.[39] South Africa has tried to cut off such outside assistance through financial curbs, but the churches have successfully resisted. The government has been able to generate support against sanctions from the evangelical churches, Buthelezi's political group, and the Inkatha and Inkatha-based trade unions.[40] But strong internal support for sanctions of various kinds has come from the South African Council of Churches, Catholic bishops, and the Congress of South African Trade Unions, which have been given external assistance in a remarkable display of solidarity.[41]

To be able to evoke international sanctions against their own government is a new tactic for most social change movements. The fact that in South Africa these movements are nonviolent is a major distinction. They have sought to bring about change through peaceful civil disobedience, although violence has occurred. In the face of such widespread repression, this courageous spirit has given the movement much credibility in the Western world.

Of course, there are links between the same external support groups and governments and the ANC, which engaged in armed struggle but also advocated sanctions. But they see it as a dual strategy that broadens the attack on the apartheid structure. The moderate wing under Oliver Tambo controlled the ANC in exile and sought negotiation rather than a military outcome.[42]

A younger, militant group in the ANC has little faith in the effectiveness of sanctions or the integrity of the Western powers who pretend to engage in them.[43] However, they are increasingly isolated as the coalition of forces in South Africa and outside has grown among Africans and minorities for a negotiated settlement on terms that have been specified as the end of emergency laws, release of all political prisoners, and the termination of apartheid.[44] These groups support international sanctions as a major instrument, together with armed struggle, for bringing about an acceptance on all sides of peace as the basis for proceeding to discuss the basis for a fair and equitable settlement. Extreme groups on both sides oppose these negotiations for a settlement on ideological grounds, as they did over Rhodesia.

Today these dissenters have less support since the Soviet Union, under Gorbachev, has supported South Africa over settlement of the conflict through negotiations.[45] And the U.S. State Department has publicly stated the terms for beginning negotiations.[46]

INTERNAL NEGOTIATIONS FORCED BY SANCTIONS

Merle Lipton, among others, considers that the movement toward "reform" in South Africa has been more the result of internal political decisions than the result of sanctions.[47] This is probably true; but it fails to note the importance of sanctions. This view maintains that the right-wing backlash is fueled by external pressures, and if the level of sanctions is raised it could mean that the "Verkramptes" will defeat the reform movement. Particularly feared are the Afrikaner Weerstands Beweging (AWB), led by Terre Blanche, who are paramilitary, and the White Wolves, who are a "secret disappearances" group. This view is one-sided as it neglects the importance of the new democratic interracial left and its growing alliance with Africans.

Since the 1980s there has been a marked shift to the right in South African white politics. But most South African analysts consider this to be more the result of the rising conflict and violence in South Africa between Africans and the police and between African factions than as the result of external pressures of antiapartheid or sanctions.

The impact of sanctions on the white population has clearly accelerated division. This division of the ruling class has hastened settlement by strengthening the antiapartheid groups. Sanctions have divided the new industrialists from the farmers of the Transvaal, and the predominantly English-speaking South Africans of the Cape Province and Natal from the Verkrampte of the Orange Free State. This has given impetus to the Verlichte within the National Party.[48]

There has been a liberal defection as well, represented by Dennis Worral, former ambassador to the UK, and the Institute for Democratic Alternatives.

The September 6, 1989, elections gave strong support to this thesis of the emergence of a broad antiapartheid coalition in opposition to the threat from the apartheid right. While the conservatives increased their seats in the National Parliament, the newly formed Democratic Party, which is liberal and antiapartheid, also gained.[49] The National Party was forced to choose which direction it would follow to protect its declining majority. The new leadership under President F. W. de Klerk has decided to go in the direction of the Democrats and the opening of serious negotiations with the African majority. The authorization of peaceful demonstrations[50] by the black-led mass democratic movement was an early indication that many changes in the repression of the government were to come. Frederick Van Zyl Slabbert has argued that the right wing is not a threat "if you make the world, national politics, that is, include the Africans."[51] He believes the liberal whites will find a powerful majority with the Africans, though this will not be done easily. Nelson Mandela has made a similar argument that a coalition of the Verlichte whites and the ANC has little to fear from the relatively small right wing.

There is a trend within the National Party itself toward a wider circle of negotiation that will attempt to bring African leaders into the government. The president, F. W. de Klerk, has been reported to have eased Botha out not only for health and age reasons, but also because he was unable to move, as they put it, toward a new South Africa.[52] This, some observers believe, brought about in 1990 genuine discussions with Mandela and the ANC as well as other Africans like Buthelezi. The report of the South African Law Commission that came during this transition presented the basis for such a major step. It called for a bill of rights for all racial groups and unrestricted franchise.[53] This is clearly an alternative direction for South Africa to move in, with the help of African leaders and some accommodation among them. Such a coalition of Verlichtes, Democrats, UDF, ANC, etc., would not be vulnerable to the racists of the right.

There are enormous problems to be worked out, such as the relationship with the ANC leadership and the Inkatha in Natal led by Gatsha Buthelezi. The position of the homeland leaders is surprisingly supportive of Mandela. Obviously, these traditional leaders have many differences with the urban-based UDF and the ANC. The ANC made it clear that negotiations would only seriously begin after conditions have been met: (1) the release of all political prisoners, (2) the end of the emergency laws, (3) repatriation of exiles, (4) repeal of apartheid laws, and (5) removal of troops from the townships.[54] By mid-1990 most of these conditions had been met, and negotiations were well underway. Mandela bridges many of these differences as he is both a traditional and a modern leader and is idolized by the African population as a whole.

The conservative whites have grown in strength. However, the far right whites will be dealt with in terms of force if they resort to force in attacking the government. The government has said bombings, disappearances, and assassination attempts against the opposition cannot be tolerated. However, retaining the loyalty of the security police and military is a critical aspect of such a transition. There are reports that this loyalty has eroded in recent years.[55]

SANCTIONS IMPACT

The negotiation process has been facilitated by sanctions from the outside. If we are looking only at white politics, we get a skewed picture. The enhancement of black political consciousness and its ability to create new space and forms of operation with the South African repressive system clearly has had reciprocal effects on white politics. Sanctions, it has been shown, are an integral part of that growth of the critical social movement among Africans and it can be seen as a part of the movement toward liberal politics of the white leadership and particularly in the faith community of the South African Council of Churches and the Dutch Reformed Church.[56] Sanctions have clearly played a role in all this, as the U.S. State Department now concedes.[57] If we are only looking at certain groups like the blue-collar workers among the whites, obviously sanctions have threatened their jobs and standard of living.[58] But the effect upon the owners of finance, professional classes, and the technocratic elite of the Nationalist Party has been to show them that if South Africa is to grow economically and take advantage of the new technological age, they must make accommodation with the African majority.[59] This is not only because of the growing capacity of trade unions to strike, but also because the West is set on a course of economic deprivation that is increasingly costly, resulting in technological loss as well as capital flight at a time when they are competing for world markets with other sources of semi-processed raw materials and agriculture.[60] The emergence of the European Community and the entry of the USSR into world markets, as well as the competition with North America, has become a part of the growing rival interests South Africa faces.

Nor can South Africa tell how far these embargoes may now go in cutting off their energy supply and closing their markets.[61] Attempts at sanctions bursting have been widely noted,[62] but they are marginal to an economy that is in the last analysis highly dependent and at the point of either "take off" or sharp recession. The argument that John Osborn and the Federal Chamber of Commerce and Industry (FCI) have made that in the end the South African economy is becoming more self-reliant and better able to deal with the world market has not convinced the financial market.[63] South Africa, as many of its industrial and financial leaders have said, has run out of time in the face of growing world sanctions.

EXTERNAL DECISION ON SANCTIONS

The world is set on a course of maintaining sanctions against South Africa until apartheid is dismantled and enfranchisement of the majority population takes place. This will take time, because change is coming very slowly. Threats of a right-wing takeover, or a growing trend to the right if the South African government slows negotiations and accelerates repression, will increase international demands for wider pressures. The United States has surprisingly moved into the major leadership position for the West,[64] primarily because the initiative is in the hands of the leaders of the critical social movement. If de Klerk fails, the United States will be forced to carry the European Community, the Commonwealth, and Japan into a multilateral campaign of wider sanctions. The role of the Commonwealth has been greatly diluted by Mrs. Thatcher's dominant role. However, should there be a Labour government in England in the next two years, growing voices of influence could implement the strongly worded Commonwealth Panel of Experts report. This report suggested that several major new sanctions measures be implemented, such as the non-rollover of loans and an embargo of oil supplies, if South Africa does not end apartheid.[65]

Leaders like Thatcher and Reagan have attempted to derail earlier demands with limited success. The Bush administration is caught in a dilemma: it shares many of the security reservations of the Reagan administration and respects de Klerk's intentions, but it is more receptive to human rights issues and the positions of critical social movements within the United States. The Bush administration is searching, as Stephen Davis pointed out, for accommodation with Congress and the liberals,[66] who have become more articulate on these issues than has the radical right. This is due in part to the lessening force of the Cold War and the readiness of the USSR to work out agreements, especially in parts of the world where they have low levels of security concerns. Moreover, the Bush administration does not want to replicate in South Africa the failure of the Reagan policies in Central America, especially Iran-Contra.[67]

After the positive response to the Mandela visit, the United States and other Western powers have agreed to maintain pressure, through sanctions and other diplomatic means, for a fair and acceptable role for Africans in the political economic system. Attempts to end sanctions before an equitable settlement will not succeed, as external powers will use all the limited leverage they have to reach a sustainable agreement.

Should there be a breakdown or even a setback in the negotiations, demands will be raised immediately throughout the world for increased sanctions. These sanctions would move in the directions outlined by Ved Nanda and Sanford Wright in Chapters 1 and 3 of this book. The success of the Namibian settlement has demonstrated how international pressures can facilitate a negotiated result. In the case of South Africa, these pressures are more indirect, but there is general consensus on the minimal threshold of human rights to be adopted by South Africa before the removal of sanctions. This is simply the end of apartheid, which means majority and democratic government with human rights for all.

There is an informal global system of pressure that has emerged out of the 40 years of growing NGO and governmental intervention on behalf of human rights. This new international regime of negotiation maintains the framework needed to achieve settlement.

After critical social movements reach a certain historical point of impetus, their strategies cannot be turned off or on by political leaders or their governments. This often results in rough justice, as was the case in the American Civil War, or for that matter, the Cromwellian and French Revolutions. The lesson is to create democracies that are sufficiently representative to be able to respond to nonviolent policies for structural change rather than allow continuous deterioration. The role of international human rights policy also needs to be recognized. To date, Western democracies have given little more than token recognition to the world antiapartheid movement and have only reluctantly acceded to the increasing sanctions campaign against South Africa.

The role of national and international NGOs in the negotiation process will continue to be more decisive than that of most governments. Their positive support for Mandela and the ANC over the years has greatly strengthened the weaker position. Right-wing nationalist groups have attempted to undercut any movement toward a peaceful negotiated settlement. But major governments appear to have shifted in favor of democratic, negotiated settlements in many outstanding world disputes. The case of South Africa has been a difficult and tragic one, but it is rapidly becoming a historical landmark in the emergence of a more peaceful and just world.

NOTES

1. One of the best summaries of this view for international relations is R. B. J. Walker's *One World, Many Worlds: Struggles for a Just World Peace* (Boulder, Colo.: Lynne Reinner, 1988), 80.

2. Paul C. Lauren, *Power and Prejudice: The Politics of Diplomacy of Racial Discrimination* (Boulder, Colo.: Westview Press, 1988), 233–234.

3. A survey and documentation of these is provided by the Association for Elimination of All Forms of Racial Discrimination (EAFORD), which publishes occasional papers and the biannual *Without Prejudice*, Washington, D.C.

4. See George W. Shepherd, *Anti-Apartheid* (Westport, Conn.: Greenwood, 1977).

5. Lauren, *Power and Prejudice*, 249.

6. Joseph Hanlon and Roger Omond, *The Sanctions Handbook* (New York: Penguin Books, 1987): "Somehow the means had become confused with the ends—the strategy had become the goal itself" (p. 55).

7. Advocates of nonviolent action like the Fellowship of Reconciliation (FOR) and NAACP have been in the forefront of sanctions policies.

8. Quoted in "U.S. Business in South Africa: Voices for Withdrawal," *Southern African Perspectives* (New York: Africa Fund), 1983.

9. *New York Times*, April 17, 1981.

10. "Sanctions," The Africa Fund, June 19, 1986.

11. For example, the president of the OAU in 1986, Abdou Diouf of Senegal, told the PLO that the world's workers should unite to end investments in South Africa. *New York Times*, June 19, 1986.

12. Randall Robinson, executive director of Trans-Africa, stated, "We believe without qualification, that the United States should unilaterally totally disinvest its corporate money and break all connection with South Africa." *Africa News*, September 1980.

13. Elna Schoeman, *South African Sanctions Directory, 1946–1988*, "Actions by Governments, Banks, Churches, Trade Unions, Universities, International and Regional Organizations" (Johannesburg: South African Institute of International Affairs, 1988), Bibliography Series, No. 18, pp. 1–7.

14. Ronald Segal, *Sanctions against South Africa* (Baltimore: Penguin, 1964).

15. U.N. Security Council Res. No. 418, Nov. 1977. An earlier voluntary ban had been adopted in 1963.

16. *Transnational Corporations in South Africa and Namibia: United Nations Public Hearings*, Vol. 3 (New York: 1987) 308–316.

17. Janice Love, *The United States Anti-Apartheid Movement* (New York: Praeger, 1985).

18. See Appendix A.

19. See Appendix A.

20. The United States and the United Kingdom have continued to veto attempts at mandatory U.N. multilateral economic sanctions against South Africa (see S.C. Res., Mar. 1988).

21. See Appendix A.

22. See the Findings of the Commonwealth Eminent Persons Group on Southern Africa, *Mission to South Africa* (London: Penguin Books, 1980), 53–54.

23. U.S. Congress Comprehensive Anti-Apartheid Act of 1986 (Washington, D.C.: GPO, 1986).

24. The Commonwealth members agreed to ban government loans, procurement, trade missions, and contracts; prohibit imports of gold coins, uranium, coal, iron, and steel; embargo oil, nuclear technology, and computers for security use; ban cultural and scientific links; terminate double-taxation agreements; sever air links; stop bank loans, new investments, and tourist promotion; the U.K. agreed only to advise no new investment and to ban iron, steel, and gold coins. *Africa Research Bulletin*, pp. 8310–8313 (Economic Series).

25. The European Community only agreed in principle to banning iron and steel. They resisted a ban on coal, oil, and new investment, and bans were voluntary. *European Communities Official Journal*, September 19, 1986; October 31, 1986.

26. Merle Lipton summarizes these points in her seminal study. *Sanctions and South Africa: The Dynamics of Economic Isolation*, Special Report No. 1119, January 1988. *Economist* (Intelligence Unit), London, pp. 12–17.

27. Thomas L. Friedman, "White House Consults Congress on a More Effective Pretoria Policy," *New York Times*, June 28, 1989.

28. Quoted in Lipton, p. 110.

29. Walker, op. cit., p. 80.

30. John Brewer, *After Soweto: An Unfinished Journey* (Oxford: Clarendon Press, 1987).

31. Heribert Adam, *Modernizing Racial Dominance* (Berkeley and Los Angeles: University of California Press, 1971); John Saul and Stephen Gelb, *The Crisis in South Africa* (New York: Monthly Review Press, 1986).

32. Gail Gerhart, *Black Power in South Africa* (Berkely and Los Angeles: University of California Press, 1978).

33. Brewer, op. cit., p. 19.

34. Various and conflicting polls have been issued, but they all showed Mandela the clear favorite of Africans. *Sunday Times* (London), August 1985.

35. Support for sanctions is less clear. The London *Sunday Times* poll in August 1985 showed 77 percent of blacks for sanctions. But Lipton reports more recent results that show this has slipped and support has shifted to selective disinvestment. Lipton, op. cit., p. 119. Polls are deceptive, especially in the South African context.

36. Mandela maintained this position in mid-1990 in his visit to the West, especially the United States, "Mandela Will Not Renounce Force Now," *New York Times*, June 26, 1990.

37. Bishop Desmond M. Tutu, "Sanctions v. Apartheid," *New York Times*, June 16, 1986.

38. Corporate pressure for reform, i.e., trade union recognition, has been in part to head off demands for sanctions and disinvestment. But it has benefited the strengthening of trade unions in COSATU.

39. See Charles Villa-VinCio, "Ways of Being Church in South Africa," *Christianity and Crisis* 48, no. 19 (January 19, 1989): 462–465; and Khoza E. Mgojo, "The Church in Action in South Africa," *Africa Today* 36, no. 1 (1988): 23–29.

A fine expression of this is Allan Boesak's *Farewell to Innocence: A Socio-Ethical Study on Black Theology and Black Power* (Maryknoll: Orbis Books, 1977).

40. Dr. Mongosuthur Buthelezi, "Sanctions: Why I Cannot Support Them," *Clarion Call* vol. 3 (1988), Bureau of Communications, Kwazulu Government. This publication also reports much opposition to sanctions among Pentecostal and Afrikaner churches, led by the Rev. M. L. Badenhorst, president of the Full Gospel Church of God (p. 42).

41. Some of these private sources of assistance that are church-based and antiapartheid have been channeled through such groups as the Africa Fund

in New York and the International Defense and Aid Fund in London. The World Council of Churches in Geneva has provided funds directly to external movements, such as the ANC and SWAPO.

42. Joseph Llelyveld, "Black Challenge to Pretoria," *New York Times*, October 12, 1983.

43. Stephen Davis, *Apartheid Rebels* (New Haven: Yale University Press, 1987), 208–209.

44. William Claiborne, *Washington Post*, May 7, 1989.

45. Peter Younghusband, *Washington Times*, May 21, 1989.

46. Robert Pear, *New York Times*, September 8, 1989.

47. Lipton, op. cit., pp. 114–115.

48. Timothy D. Sisk, "White Politics in South Africa," *Africa Today* 36, no. 1 (1989): 36. Sisk quotes a University of Stellenbosh philosopher who sees the NP divided between 30 percent Verlichte, and 30 percent Verkrampte, and 40 percent in-between (p. 37).

49. The Democratic Party was formed in 1988 out of the failing Progressive-Federal Party and two small liberal coalitions in Parliament. Its leaders are Wynend Malan and Dennis Worral, who head a group of 33 Democrats opposed to 39 Conservatives. *New York Times*, September 8, 1989.

50. *New York Times*, September 11, 1989.

51. Frederick Van Zyl Slabbert (interview with Margaret No Vicki), *Africa Report* (Jan.-Feb. 1989): 34.

52. Christopher Wren, *New York Times*, March 7, 1989.

53. Christopher Wren, *New York Times*, March 12, 1989.

54. William Claiborne, *Washington Post*, May 5, 1989.

55. Kenneth Grundy reported on earlier phases of this in *The Militarization of South African Politics* (Bloomington: Indian University Press, 1986).

56. Johan Heyns, professor and leader of the largest Dutch Reformed Church, led his church to recognize that apartheid was based on "scriptural error" in 1986 and in 1989 to call for Mandela's release "without renouncing violence." *New York Times*, March 3, 1989.

57. *Wall Street Journal*, June 30, 1987.

58. Charles Becker, "Impact of Sanctions on South Africa," *African Studies Review* 31, no. 2 (1989): 83–84.

59. Haider Ali Khan, "Measuring and Analyzing the Economic Effects of Trade Sanctions against South Africa: A New Aapproach," *Africa Today* 33, no. 2–3 (1986): 47–59. See also his *The Political Economy of Sanctions against Apartheid* (Boulder, Colo.: Lynne Reinner, 1989), 76.

60. Lipton, op. cit.

61. The Moorsan and Becker Studies both see the oil embargo and a gold ban as having significant impact as selective sanctions. Gold is difficult to enforce but would heavily affect South Africa's foreign exchange position. See Richard Moorsan, *The Scope for Sanctions* (London: Catholic Institute for International Relations, 1989), 34–35.

62. For example, "West Germany/South Africa: Secret Ships Deal Goes Ahead," *African Confidential* 29, no. 6 (March 18, 1988).

63. Lipton, p. 101.

64. *Wall Street Journal*, June 30, 1989.

65. *Commonwealth Expert /Study on Sanctions*, headed by Joseph Hanlon (London: Commonwealth of Nations, 1989).

66. Robert Pear, *New York Times*, Sept. 8, 1989.

67. The new Asst. Secretary of State, Herman Cohen, requested South Africa be given time under President de Klerk to make reforms. *New York Times*, June 25, 1989.

Chronology of Arms Embargoes against South Africa

_____Timothy U. Mozia_____

UNITED NATIONS ARMS EMBARGOES

Resolution	Date	Particulars
General Assembly (GA) Resolution (Res.) 1761 (XVII).	Nov. 6, 1962	Member states, separately or collectively, to refrain from exporting goods—all arms and ammunition —to South Africa (SA); calls on Security Council (SC) to impose arms embargo against SA.
SC Res. 181	Aug. 7, 1963	Voluntary arms embargo against SA; all states to cease sale and shipment of arms, ammunition of all types, and military vehicles to SA.
SC Res. 182	Dec. 4, 1963	Embargo broadened to include sale and shipment of all types of ammunition, arms, military vehicles and equipment, and materials for the manufacture and maintenance of arms and ammunition in SA.
SC Res. 191	June 16, 1964	Reaffirmation of SC Res. 181 and SC Res. 182.
SC Res. 282	July 23, 1970	Call on all member states to revoke all licenses and military patents granted the SA government or to

Resolution	Date	Particulars
		SA companies for the manufacture of arms and ammunition, aircraft and naval craft, or other military vehicles; prohibition of investment in, or technical assistance for the manufacture of those items.
SC Res. 418	Nov. 4, 1977	Acting under chapter 7 of the U.N. Charter, the SC determined that "the acquistition by SA of arms and related *materiel* constituted a threat to the maintenance of international peace and security"; mandatory arms embargo imposed against SA; call on states to comply with SC Res. 181 and SC Res. 182 in terms of cessation of sale and transfer of arms and related materiel of all types, including assistance geared toward the manufacture and development of nuclear weapons; member states to review all contracts made with SA for the manufacture and maintenance of arms and related materiel with a view to terminating them.
SC Res. 421	Dec. 9, 1977	Committee established by the SC to search for ways of making the embargo more effective.
ECOSOC Res. 1978/73	Aug. 4, 1978	Economic and Social Council calls on states to refrain from all activities that might directly or indirectly strengthen SA's military capability.
SC Res. 473	June 13, 1980	Call for effective implementation of SC Res. 418 and the need for the enactment of effective national legislation for that purpose.
GA Res. 36/172 D	Dec. 17, 1981	Call on all governments that had not yet done so to implement the arms embargo against SA and prohibit all forms of nuclear collaboration with SA.
GA Res. 37/69 D	Dec. 9, 1982	Condemnation of the actions of Multinational Corporations that continue to enhance the military and nuclear capabilities of SA through their collaboration with the SA regime.

Resolution	Date	Particulars
GA Res. 38/39 G	Dec. 5, 1983	Call on all member states to prohibit all military and nuclear cooperation with SA. This includes governments, corporations, and individuals within these states.
GA Res. 39/72 A	Dec. 13, 1984	Substance of GA Res. 38/39 G reiterated.
SC Res. 558	Dec. 13, 1984	States to refrain from importing arms, ammunition, and military vehicles produced in SA.

ARMS EMBARGOES BY COUNTRY

Australia

Date	Source	Particulars
June 1985	Government statement	Under the Customs (Prohibited) Export Regulations, export of all arms to SA is prohibited without the authority of the Minister of Defense.
Aug. 19, 1985	Foreign Minister William Hayden	Prohibition of exports of computer hardware and any other products known to be of use to the SA security forces; ban on the importation of arms, ammunition, and military vehicles from SA; and the prohibition of all export of arms to SA.
Aug. 21, 1985	Australian document to GA A40/565-S/17411	Notification of reaffirmation of Aug. 19 statement to GA by Foreign Minister Hayden.

Austria

Sept. 25, 1985	Federal Ministry of Foreign Affairs statement to the 40th session of the GA	Prohibit all export of computer equipment that may be used by the SA police; prohibit the participation of public enterprises in SA nuclear procurement procedures.

Bahamas

Date	Source	Particulars
April 18, 1985	Goverment statement on GA Res. 39/50 A & B	Support for a mandatory arms embargo against SA.

Barbados

Feb. 1986	Government statement on GA Res. 40/64 A & I	No relations with SA in *all* facets.

Belgium

Aug. 8, 1979	Government statement to SC	Voluntary embargo on the provision of arms to SA since 1963.

Botswana

Feb. 1986	Government statement on GA Res. 40/64 A & B	No military and nuclear dealings with SA.

Brazil

Aug. 9, 1985	Presidential degree	Conformity with 1977 U.N. arms embargo.
April 1986	Government statement on GA Res. 40/64 A & I	Ban on sale of arms and related materiel to SA; prohibition of shipment and transhipment of same throughout Brazilian territory.

Bulgaria

June 24, 1985	Government statement on GA Res. 39/50 A & B	Call for *total* international isolation of SA; no relations whatsoever with SA.

Canada

Nov. 15, 1983	Government reply to U.N. secretary-general	Voluntary embargo on sale of arms and military equipment to SA since 1963; embargo broadened to include spare parts in 1970; support for mandatory arms embargo in 1977; court action taken at times to ensure strict implementation, such as

Date	Source	Particulars
		charges laid against a Canadian firm, Space Research Corporation, for violating Canada's Export and Import Permits Act through shipment of arms to SA and the falsification of documents in the process.
July 6, 1985	Statement by Secretary of State for External Affairs Joe Clark	Tightening of the application of the U.N. arms embargo through restrictions on the export of sensitive equipment like computers to the SA police, armed forces, and related agencies; enforcement of U.N. arms embargo on the importation of SA manufactured goods.
Sept. 13, 1985	Joe Clark	Reemphasized above.

China

Date	Source	Particulars
March 1985	Government statement on GA Res. 39/50 A & B	The Chinese government will not enter into any military contacts with SA.
Aug. 1985	Government statement on SC Res. 418	Strictly abided by and implemented the resolution.

Czechoslovakia

Date	Source	Particulars
June 1985	Government statement on GA Res. 39/50 A & B	No relations with SA; participates in activities aimed at all-round isolation, such as in the military sphere.
Feb. 1986	Government statement on GA Res. 40/64 A & I	No military relations with SA.

Denmark

Date	Source	Particulars
Feb. 10, 1978	Government reply to U.N. secretary-general	Adopted on February 10, 1978, legislation that prohibits the "sale, transfer or provision to SA of arms, weapons, war materials, ammunition of all types, military vehicles and equipment,

Date	Source	Particulars
		paramilitary police equipment, and spare parts; the provision of components and materials for the manufacture of the above; grants of licensing arrangements for the manufacture and maintenance of the above; and refusal to cooperate with SA in the nuclear field.
May 28, 1984	Resolutions on sanctions tightening by the Danish parliament	Stressed the commitment of the Danish government to ensure the realization of the U.N. SC arms embargo against SA.
Aug. 1985	Government statement on SC Res. 418	Prohibition of the sale, transfer, or attempt to transfer or sell arms, weapons, war materials, or related materials of all types; military vehicles and equipment; spare parts or licensing agreements with SA for the manufacture of the above; collaboration with SA in the nuclear field; and the conviction of persons found guilty of infringing the above embargoes.
Feb. 1986	Government statement on GA Res. 40/64 A & I	Denmark observes the ban on military imports from SA imposed by SC Res. 558 of 1984 and favors an extension and strengthening of the arms embargo.

France

Date	Source	Particulars
July 24, 1985	Prime minister	Frances will abide by SC Res. 558.
Jan. 9, 1986	Decree 86-34	Prohibition of exports, reexports, and imports of a paramilitary nature destined for or coming from SA; export and reexport of materiel intended for operations in nuclear installations subject to the issuance of a license; those materiels capable of being used to maintain order in SA are to be subject to the issuance of a license within the framework of the

Date	Source	Particulars
		Nov. 30, 1944 decree. Such licenses shall not be granted "as soon as it is established that the *materiel* is intended for use in maintaining order." Those intended for use in nuclear installations are also subject to the issuance of a license in accordance with the above-mentioned decree.

Germany, East

Date	Source	Particulars
Aug. 1985	Government statement on SC Res. 418	Welcomes the resolution and strictly abides by its provisions.
Feb. 1986	Governmnent statement on GA Res. 40/64 A & I	Reiteration of the above; allusion to the necessity, in future, to close all gaps still existing in the arms embargo imposed against SA.

Germany, West

Date	Source	Particulars
July 1986	Government statement	Rigorously controlled embargo on the export of arms and paramilitary equipment to SA; prohibition of exports of sensitive equipment destined for the police and armed forces in SA; refusal to cooperate with SA in the military sphere; and the prohibition of collaboration with SA in the nuclear sector.

Israel

Date	Source	Particulars
Dec. 7, 1977 & April 1978	Government statement	Undertook to comply with U.N. SC Res. 418.

Italy

Date	Source	Particulars
1972	Government statement	Amendment of law prohibiting export of military aircraft without government authorization, to include export of civilian aircraft to SA.

Date	Source	Particulars
May 3, 1986	Government statement	No specific legislation concerning the sale of arms and other sensitive products to SA; all requests for authorization to export arms determined on a case by case basis by a special committee presided over by the Foreign Trade Minister. Such requests have been rejected as a matter of course since 1972.

Japan

July 1986	Government statement	Absolutely no military cooperation between Japan and SA; no exchange of personnel; strict observance of U.N. arms embargo; and no cooperation with SA in the field of nuclear development.

Kampuchea

Feb. 1986	Government statement on GA Res. 40164	Supports U.N. arms embargo against SA and calls for more stringent sanctions by the developed countries—His Royal Highness, Samdech Norodon Sihanouk.

Libya

Aug. 1985	Government statement on SC Res. 418	Full commitment to boycott SA in all military aspects.

Netherlands

Aug. 1985	Government statement	Respect for, and strict observance of U.N. arms embargoes against SA; legislation to that effect based on the Import and Export Act of 1962, Strategic Goods Decree of 1963, the Sanctions Act of 1977, the Sanctions Decree (Transportation of Arms to SA) of 1981, and the Sanctions Decree

Date	Source	Particulars
		(License to SA) of 1981, which prohibits military relations of any kind with SA; no government consent is given for transactions involving military goods for SA.

Norway

Date	Source	Particulars
June 1985	Government statement on GA Res. 39/72 G	The U.N. arms embargo against SA should be strengthened to include equipment designed for dual purposes (civilian/military); observance of all U.N. arms embargoes.
Aug. 1985	Government statement on SC Res. 418	Prohibition of export or delivery of war material and any kind of similar material to SA; illegal to export equipment and supplies for production and maintenance of war materials to SA; and prohibition of nuclear cooperation with SA.

Poland

Date	Source	Particulars
April 15, 1985	Government statement on GA Res. 39/50 A & B	Supports the total international isolation of SA in the military sphere, among others, and favors mandatory sanctions against SA under chapter 7 of the U.N. Charter.

Romania

Date	Source	Particulars
Aug. 1985	Government statement on SC Res. 418	Actively participated in working out and adopting this resolution, observes and supports it, supported and is supporting the demands, particularly of African countries, on the strengthening and expansion of the arms embargo against SA.

Sweden

Date	Source	Particulars
1985	Act on Prohibition of Investments in SA & Namibia	Sweden already imposed an arms embargo against SA before the decision of the United Nation to do so in 1977; legislation passed in 1977

Date	Source	Particulars
		prohibits export of arms and related material. This was extended in 1985 to cover exports of data-processing equipment and related software, as well as cross-country vehicles and fuel for such vehicles.
June 1985	Government statement on GA Res. 39/72 G	In 1983, Sweden passed legislation prohibiting the importation of arms and related material from SA. Above measures were also reemphasized.

Syria

Date	Source	Particulars
Feb. 1986	Government statement on GA Res. 40/64 A & I	Support for full application of arms embargo against SA under the auspices of the United Nations.

Thailand

Date	Source	Particulars
June 1985	Government statement on SC Res. 418	Initiation of regulations imposing arms embargo against SA as per SC Res. 418.

United Kingdom

Date	Source	Particulars
1985	Excerpts from the Export of Goods (Control) Order 1985 S.I.1985 No. 849	Prohibition of the export and import of military aircraft, arms, and related material, ammunition, military wares and appliances, and security and paramilitary and police equipment.
Sept. 25, 1985	Statement by Foreign and Commonwealth Office Spokesman	A rigorously controlled embargo on the importation of arms and paramilitary equipment from SA; support for SC Res. 558; refusal to cooperate in the military sphere with SA; and the recall of military attachés accredited to SA.

USA

Date	Source	Particulars
1963	UN document ST/CTC/84, 1986	Voluntary arms embargo.

Date	Source	Particulars
1977	USA Office of Federal Register, Code of Federal Regulations, vol. 15, pts. 300-399, revised January 1, 1983	Acceptance of U.N. mandatory arms embargo; no sale of arms or related material, and a ban on the export of any goods to the SA military and police; purchasers of U.S. exports of the embargoed items required to certify that they will not be reexported to SA.
Sept. 9, 1985	Presidential statement	Ban on all computer exports to SA; prohibition on exports of nuclear goods or technology to SA except as is required to implement nuclear proliferation safeguards of the International Atomic Energy Agency or those necessary to protect health and safety.
Oct. 1986	Comprehensive Anti-Apartheid Act	Prohibition of imports of military equipment from SA, including arms, military vehicles, or manufacturing data for such activities; prohibition of military assistance to countries that are identified as circumventing the international arms embargo against SA; prohibition of nuclear trade, export of computers, computer software, or goods and technology intended to manufacture or service computers used by the military police or any SA security systems; and items included in the U.S. munitions list. This does not include goods not covered by SC Res. 418. The president, in case of goods exported for commercial usage, must notify Congress accordingly and demonstrate that they are not for military use.

USSR

Aug. 10, 1985	Government statement on SC Res. 418	Strict observance of SC Res. 418 and 472 relating to arms embargo against SA, and Res. 558 concerning the importation of arms, ammunition of all types, and military vehicles produced in SA.

Date	Source	Particulars
Feb. 1986	Government state-ment on GA Res. 40/64 A & I	Reaffirmation of above; need for strict compliance with above; condemns U.S. policy of con-structive engagement and "active collaboration" of USA and other Western countries with SA.

Yugoslavia

Feb. 1986	Government state-ment on GA Res. 40/64 A & I	Yugoslavia has supported and im-plemented a comprehensive and complete boycott of SA in all fields of international coopera-tion, including the military.

Chronology of Economic Embargoes against South Africa

_____*Timothy U. Mozia*_____

UNITED NATIONS ECONOMIC EMBARGOES

Resolution	Date	Particulars
GA 1761 (XVII)	Nov. 6, 1962	Member states, separately or collectively, to close their ports to vessels flying the SA flag; enact legislation prohibiting their ships from entering SA ports; refuse landing and passage facilities to all aircraft belonging to the SA government and companies; and refrain from exporting goods to SA.
GA 2054 A (XX)	Dec. 15, 1965	Appeal to SA's major trading partners to cease colloration with SA.
GA 2202 A (XXI)	Dec. 16, 1966	States called upon to discourage the establishment of closer economic and financial relations with SA, especially in the realms of investment and trade; discourage loans by banks in their countries to the SA government or private concerns.
GA 2506 B (XXIV)	Nov. 21, 1969	All states enjoined to refrain from extending loans, investment, and technical assistance to the

Resolution	Date	Particulars
		SA government and companies registered in SA; take measures to dissuade SA's main trading partners from doing business with SA.
GA 2923 E (XXVII)	Nov. 15, 1972	Members of international agencies and organizations, especially EEC members, GATT, and IMF, to deny all commercial assistance to SA and refrain from extending facilities to SA.
GA 3151 G. (XXVIII)	Dec. 14, 1973	Call on states that had not yet done so to close trade promotion offices in SA; deny facilities for offices of SA trade commissioners; terminate all tariff preferences to SA; refuse any credits for trade with SA guarantees for investment in SA.
GA 3411 G. (XXX)	Dec. 10, 1975	Condemned the action of states still collaborating with SA in the economic sphere.
GA 31/6 H	Nov. 9, 1976	All states to prohibit loans to, or investment in SA by banks or corporations within their national jurisdiction; condemnation of Transnational Corporations (TNCs) that continue to intensify their activities in SA.
GA 31/6 J	Nov. 9, 1976	All governments enjoined not to extend loans, investments, and technical assistance to SA, prohibit loans by banks and other financial institutions in their countries to SA; deny tariffs and other preferences to SA exports and any inducements or guarantees for investment in SA; take action in international agencies like the EEC, GATT, IMF, and IBRD for denial by them of all forms of assistance to SA; and take action singly or in coalition against TNCs collaborating with SA.

Resolution	Date	Particulars
ECOSOC 1978/73	Aug. 4, 1978	Condemned the continued investment and exploitation of black labor by the TNCs in SA; urged all TNCs to comply with relevant U.N. resolutions and for governments to take legislative, administrative, judicial, and other measures to put an end to the activities of their TNCs in SA. Also called on governments to prohibit all persons and enterprises of their nationality from making any royalty or tax payments to SA or transferring any assets or other resources to SA against the resolutions of the United Nations.
GA 33/183 H	Jan. 24, 1979	All governments called upon to prevent TNCs, banks, and all other institutions from collaborating with the SA government, terminate credits by the IMF and other financial bodies to SA, and prohibit the sale of Krugerrands.
ECOSOC 1979/75	Aug. 3, 1979	Reaffirmation of ECOSOC 1978/73.
GA 34/93 A	Dec. 12, 1979	Reiteration of GA 33/183; and all governments requested to terminate promotion of, or assistance to, trade with or investment in SA.
ECOSOC 1980/59	July 24, 1980	Reaffirmation of ECOSOC 1978/73.
GA 35/206 C	Dec. 16, 1980	Reaffirmation of GA 33/183 and GA 34/93 A.
GA 35/206 F	Dec. 17, 1981	All states that had not yet done so enjoined to comply with GA 33/183 and GA 34/93 A and to cease all forms of direct and indirect investment with SA.
ECOSOC	Oct. 27, 1982	Reaffirmation of ECOSOC 1978/73.

Resolution	Date	Particulars
GA 37/69 A	Dec. 9, 1982	Condemnation of TNCs that continued to do business with SA in the military, nuclear, petroleum, and other fields and financial institutions that continued to grant loans and credits to SA; SC urged to impose mandatory and comprehensive sanctions against SA under chapter 7 of the U.N. Charter; states that had not yet done so urged to adopt separate and collective measures for comprehensive sanctions against SA pending action by the SC.
ECOSOC 1983/74	July 29, 1983	Reaffirmation of ECOSOC 1978/73.
GA 38/39 A	Dec. 5, 1983	Reiteration of GA 37/69 A.
GA 39/72 A & G	Dec. 13, 1984	Reiteration of GA 37/69 A.
ECOSOC 1984/53	July 25, 1984	Called on all states to prevent their TNCs from doing business in SA and to prevent further new investments in SA and Namibia.
SC 566	June 19, 1985	All states that had not yet done so enjoined to take appropriate voluntary action against SA in the following spheres: stopping of new investments and the application of disincentives to that end; reexamination of maritime and aerial relations with SA; ban on SA Krugerrands and coins; and restrictions in sports and cultural realms.
SC 569	July 26, 1985	Restated SC 566 and emphasized the need for states to suspend guaranteed export of loans.
GA 40/64 A	Dec. 10, 1985	Reiteration of GA 37/69 A and the need to impose an effective embargo on the supply of oil, oil products, and oil technology to SA as well as a call for the withdrawal of investments from SA.

Resolution	Date	Particulars
U.N./OAU World Conference on Sanctions against SA	June 16-20, 1986	Recognition of the need for comprehensive mandatory sanctions and a call on the SC to adopt same.
GA 41/35	Nov. 10, 1986	Call for the total isolation of SA by all organizations within the U.N. system as well as corporations still doing business with it.

ECONOMIC EMBARGOES BY COUNTRY

Date	Source	Particulars

Australia

Date	Source	Particulars
Aug. 19, 1985	Government memo to the Panel of Eminent Persons	Suspension of all new investments in SA by government and public authorities; prohibition of all new direct investments in Australia by the SA government and its agencies; ban on the importation of SA Krugerrands and coins; prohibition of new contractual arrangements above $20,000 with SA majority-owned companies, closure of Australia's Trade Commission in Johannesburg; directive to Australian banks to suspend new loans to SA; and the introduction of a formal code of conduct to guide Australian companies with interests in SA.
Aug. 21, 1986	Parliamentary statement by prime minister	Acceptance by Australia to ban air links with SA; ban on new investments or reinvestments of profits earned in SA; ban on the import of agricultural products from SA; termination of double-taxation agreements; termination of all government assistance to investment in, and trade with SA; ban on all government procurement in SA; ban on the promotion

Date	Source	Particulars
		of tourism; ban on the importation of uranium, iron and steel from SA; and the reduction of SA consular representation in Australia through withdrawal of temporary residence authority for SA trade officers at the SA Trade Commissioner's Office at Melbourne.
Oct. 31, 1986	Foreign Minister William Hayden	Termination of Air Services Agreement with SA effective October 31, 1987.

Austria

Sept. 26, 1985	Federal Ministry of Foreign Affairs	Suspension of all investments by Austrian public enterprises in SA; ban on importation of SA Krugerrands and coins; imposition of restrictions in the field of sports and cultural relations; stoppage of government guarantees for export credits until further notice; and the prohibition of the export of computers that could be used by the SA military and police.

Bulgaria

June 24, 1985	Government statement	Called for the imposition of comprehensive mandatory sanctions against SA under chapter 7 of the U.N. Charter.

Canada

Nov. 15, 1983	Government statement	Termination, since 1977, of programs that encouraged or promoted trade and investments in SA; withdrawal of Canadian Trade Commissioners previously assigned to SA; closure of the Consulate-General at Johannesburg; suspension of the use of Export Development Corporation's (EDC) government account

Date	Source	Particulars
		for financing and insuring trade with SA; suspension of the EDC's corporate account for SA in 1981.
July 6, 1985	External Affairs Secretary of State Joe Clark	Strengthening of the Voluntary Code of Conduct Concerning the Employment Practices of Canadian Companies Operating in SA; abrogation of the Canada-SA double taxation agreements; withdrawal of the Program for Export Development to Canadian exporters for market development in SA; sports boycott; and the termination of the applicability to SA of global insurance policy issued by the Export Development Corporation.
Sept. 13, 1985	External Affairs Secretary Joe Clark	Reiteration of the July 1985 speech and the introduction of a voluntary ban on loans to the SA government and its agencies; call on Canadian banks to apply such a ban; ban on the sale of crude oil and refined products to SA; embargo on air transport between Canada and SA; the opening of a register for voluntary measures taken by Canadian provinces, municipalities, private institutions, organizations, and firms against SA; allocation of $1 million on humanitarian grounds to assist the families of political prisoners and detained persons in SA; and the tripling of funds to be made available for education and training of the black community in SA.
June 12, 1986	Statement by the External Affairs Sec. of State to the Eminent Persons Group (EPG)	Ban on tourism; allocation of an additional $2 million for the education of blacks in SA; diplomatic measures like the withdrawal of the accreditation of four SA attachés for science, mining, labor, and agriculture.

China

Date	Source	Particulars
Aug. 1985	Government statement on SC Res. 418	The Chinese government has always refused to enter into relations of any kind with SA be they political, military, economic, or cultural.

Czechoslovakia

Date	Source	Particulars
Aug. 1985	Government statement on SC Res. 418	Czechoslovak authorities in charge of foreign trade management do not grant any permits for the export of goods to SA.
Feb. 1986	Government statement on GA Res. 40/64 A & I	Condemnation of member states of the United Nations still collaborating with the SA regime; no diplomatic, economic, scientific, military, cultural, or sports-related relations with SA.

Denmark

Date	Source	Particulars
May 29, 1985	Bill no. L 194 adopted by the Danish parliament	Stoppage of any new kind of investment in SA regardless of the legal form in which the investment was carried out. This, however, does not apply to investments that are made with a view to pursuing previous investments in SA. The termination of air agreements with SA was also highlighted.
Feb. 1986	Government statement on GA Res. 40/64 A & I	Recognition of the importance of mandatory sanctions as the most effective means of dismantling apartheid in SA; reiteration of the prohibition of new investments; closure of its diplomatic representation; introduction of legislation leading to a total ban on all imports of coal and a general cessation of all other imports from, and exports to SA; no exports of oil; consideration of the termination of double-taxation agreement between Denmark and SA.

Date	Source	Particulars
May 1986	Law prohibiting coal imports passed by the Danish parliament	Prohibition of coal imports from SA and contravention punishable by fine.
May 30, 1986	Law prohibiting trade with SA	Prohibition of imports of goods and services of any kind from SA.

Finland

Dec. 31, 1985	Law 1104 on Measures against SA by the Finnish parliament	Limitation of economic relations with SA as well as telecommunication and other communication; prohibition of loans and other credit; ban on conveyance of patents and manufacturing licenses to SA.

France

July 24, 1985	Prime minister	Suspension of all new investments in SA irrespective of the sector and the condition.
Jan. 9, 1986	Decree no. 86-34	Prohibition of the export and reexport of petroleum and fuel products destined for SA.

Germany, East

Feb. 1986	Government statement on GA Res. 40/64 A & I	Support for growing international demands for comprehensive sanctions under chapter 7 of the U.N. Charter; no political, economic, military, or other relations with SA; and a general abhorrence of any form of collusion with SA.

Germany, West

July 25, 1986	Government statement	Initiation of restrictive measures (arms embargoes) and positive measures such as a code of conduct, including aid to blacks, frontline states, and SADCC, which received DM 5 million in

Date	Source	Particulars
		1986. Since 1977, West Germany has only operated short-term and medium-term guarantees for exports to SA and limited such transactions to individual transactions below DM 50 million.

Japan

| July 1986 | Government statement | Distribution of U.N. resolutions to various Japanese ministries to ensure awareness and compliance; prohibition of direct investments by Japanese nationals or corporate bodies under its jurisdiction; call on Japanese banks and their branches abroad not to extend loans to SA; refrain from importing SA Krugerrands or gold coins; and increase in Japanese assistance in the area of human resources development in Southern Africa. |

Netherlands

| Feb. 1986 | Government statement on GA Res. 40/64 A & I | Declaration of support for selective mandatory sanctions against SA; support for oil embargo calls; limitation of new foreign investment and preparedness to consider unilateral action to prohibit new investment in SA provided that agreement can be reached on measures of this kind by a sufficient number of countries with economic interests in SA in order to ensure effectiveness. |

New Zealand

| Oct. 23, 1985 | Prime Minister David Lange | Support for immediate, carefully targeted, and meaningful sanctions against SA; agreement to comply with each of the economic measures that the Commonwealth decided should be applied (See British Commonwealth measures |

Date	Source	Particulars
		in the following section); willingness to move to the next stage outlined in the Commonwealth Accord and to implement the following measures: ban on air links, new investments or reinvestment of profits earned in SA, and the import of agricultural products from SA, termination of double-taxation agreements with SA, termination of all government assistance in, and trade with SA, and a ban on all government procurement in SA, government contracts with majority-owned SA companies, and on the promotion of tourism to SA.
Feb. 1986	Government statement on GA Res. 40/64 A & I	New Zealand has taken the following economic measures against SA: no import of coal from, or export to SA; prohibition of imports of SA Kruger-rands; prohibition of exports of computers to SA; no New Zealand government loans to SA; ban on government contracts for the purchase of goods originating from SA; no more export guarantee commitments to SA by the Government Export Guarantee Organization; no assistance to companies doing business with SA by the Government Export-Import Corporation; that no New Zealand companies have investments in SA; and that there is no government support for trade missions to SA.

Norway

Date	Source	Particulars
June 1985	Government statement on GA Res. 39/72 G	Support for mandatory economic sanctions against SA; Norwegian-produced oil is not sold to SA; foreign currency licenses are not granted for Norwegian investments in SA; license applications for ship exports subject to political assessment; credit guarantees not given for exports to SA; and Norwegian authorities have instructions to refrain from export-promoting activities with regard to SA.

Date	Source	Particulars
March 1987	Act on Economic Boycott against SA and Namibia	General prohibition on imports from, and exports to SA and Namibia with the exception of medicines, medical equipment, news items, printed material, or electronic, audio, and visual recordings; no carriage of crude oil by Norwegian vessels to or from SA and Namibia and by any foreign vessels at the disposal of Norwegian companies or persons domiciled in Norway; no transportation of persons to and from SA and Namibia; no loans or insurance contracts with those domiciled in SA and Namibia; no investment in or leasing of capital equipment; no transfer of patents or production rights; and a general prohibition on the organization or promotion of tourism to SA.

Poland

April 15, 1985	Government statement on GA Res. 39/50 A & B	Support for the total international isolation of SA in the political, economic, military, cultural, sports, and other fields. No relations of any sort with SA in these realms.

Romania

Aug. 1985	Government statement on SC Res. 418	No political, diplomatic, economic, or other relations with SA by all Romanian institutions and companies

Sweden

July 1979	Prohibition of Investments in SA and Namibia Act, 1979	Prohibition of new and further investments by Swedish companies or individuals in SA; those with previously existing operations to make an annual report to government; penalties for infringement to vary from a minimum of six months to two years maximum imprisonment or fine in lieu thereof.

Date	Source	Particulars
		The only exceptions to the statute are investments intended to replace worn out parts that do not involve any form of expansion.
1985	Act 98	Reiteration of the above.
June 1987	Swedish parliamentary legislation	Above prohibitions extended to imports to Sweden of goods of SA or Namibian origin; exports from Sweden to those countries; activities that might contribute to these imports and exports such as transport, loading, unloading, storage, or the provision of means to perform such activities either directly or indirectly.

Thailand

Date	Source	Particulars
June 1985	Government statement on GA Res. 39/72 G	Prohibition of bilateral trade between Thailand and SA; the imposition, since July 1978, of voluntary trade sanctions against SA.

United Kingdom

Date	Source	Particulars
1986	UN document STC/CTC/84	Voluntary ban on new investment and the promotion of tourism to SA; acceptance to implement any decision made by the EEC to prohibit imports of coal, iron and steel, and gold coins.

USA

Date	Source	Particulars
1978	Export-Import Bank (Eximbank) Amendment	Barred SA from receiving Eximbank loan guarantees pending progress away from the practice of apartheid in SA
Nov. 30, 1986		Law enacted by Congress to withhold U.S. support of IMF loans to SA or the use of its facilities by SA.

Date	Source	Particulars
Sept. 9, 1985	Statement by the president	Ban on computer exports to SA; ban on loans to SA except those that improve the economic opportunities or educational, housing, and health facilities open to SA of all races; consideration of a ban on imports of SA Krugerrands; and a ban on U.S. government assistance in the export sector to any American firm in SA employing more than 25 people that does not adhere to the comprehensive fair employment principles, especially those contained in the Sullivan Principles.
Oct. 1986	Comprehensive Anti-Apartheid Act	Prohibition of imports of SA Krugerrands and coins; ban on import of products from SA parastatal organizations, except for strategic minerals not obtainable elsewhere and vital for the economy and defense of the United States; prohibition of new loans to the SA government or the acceptance of deposits from the SA government by U.S. banks; prohibition of new investments by U.S. nationals either directly or through other entities; prohibition of imports of uranium, coal, or textiles; suspension of direct air links between the United States and SA; termination of existing double-taxation agreements; ban on imports of agricultural products, foodstuffs, iron and steel, and sugar produced in SA; empowerment of the president to limit imports of any product into the United States from another country to the extent to which such trade takes advantage of sanctions against SA. The maximum penalty for infringement was set at $1 million.

USSR

Date	Source	Particulars
June 1985	Government statement on GA Res. 39/72 G	Support for the adoption of comprehensive and mandatory sanctions against SA; no relations with SA in the economic, political, military, or any other field and accordingly, no contractual or licensing agreements with the Pretoria regime.
Feb. 1986	Government statement on GA Res. 40/64 A & B	Reiteration of the above.

Yugoslavia

Feb. 1986	Government statement on GA Res. 40/60 A & I	Yugoslavia maintains a comprehensive and complete boycott of SA in all fields of international cooperation—political, economic, cultural, sports, military, etc.

OTHER ECONOMIC EMBARGOES

Nassau (October 20, 1985): Ban on new government loans to the SA government and its agencies; readiness to probibit imports of SA Krugerrands; no government funding of trade missions to SA or for participation in exhibitions and trade fairs in SA; ban on the sale and export of oil to SA; discouragement of all cultural and scientific events in SA save for where these contribute toward the ending of apartheid. Further measures to be considered after a six-month review period are: ban on new investments or the reinvestment of profits earned in SA; ban on imports of agricultural products; termination of double-taxation agreements; termination of all government assistance for investment and trade with SA; ban on all government procurement in SA; ban on government contract with majority-owned SA companies; and a ban on the promotion of tourism to SA.

London (August 3–5, 1986)—Heads of Commonwealth State Review Meeting: Adoption of further measures to be considered after a six-month review period as stated above; ban on all new bank loans to the SA public and private sectors, ban on imports of uranium, coal, iron, and steel from SA; withdrawal of all consular representations from SA except for nationals and those of third countries to whom consular services are rendered; solicitation of the support of the international community for the implementation of these sanctions; and regret at the refusal of the British government to accede completely with the terms of the agreement.

Vancouver (October 1987)—Summit Meeting of Commonwealth States: Reiteration, with the exception of Britain, of the importance of economic sanctions; continuation of efforts to secure a more concerted application of a global sanctions program; the need to render assistance to SA neighbors, especially the frontline states; support for individual and collective efforts to increase assistance to the victims of apartheid; and commitment to a wider and tighter application of the measures agreed upon at both Nassau and London.

European Community

Luxembourg (September 10, 1985)—Ministerial Meeting of Ten EEC Members plus Spain and Portugal: Application of restrictive measures in the military sphere; cessation of oil exports to SA; and positive measures like assistance to nonviolent antiapartheid organizations such as churches; education of, and increase in levels of contact with nonwhite communities; and assistance to the SADCC and the frontline states were highlighted.

1986: Decision by the Council of Ministers to suspend imports of iron and steel from SA; prohibition of new investments and imports of gold coins from SA; and the adoption, on October 27, 1986, of the decision to suspend new direct investment in SA.

Organization of Petroleum-Exporting Countries

No transfer of petroleum to SA; no sale to parties who could reexport to SA; requirement for captains to show official papers showing ports at which they have anchored over a period of no less than one year; prohibit the loading of any vessel that has broken the embargo; support for the establishment of a center for the observation of carriers entering and leaving SA ports; coordination and exchange of information between competent marketing authorities of member states—(RE 26/5 of Ministers of Arab Petroleum Exporting Countries—May 6, 1981).

League of Arab States

Tunis (August 1984)—Conference of Arab Solidarity with the Liberation Struggle in SA: Reiterated its support for comprehensive and mandatory sanctions against SA; condemnation of U.S. constructive engagement stance, collaboration of TNCs with SA, and the close alliance between Israel and SA in the military, nuclear, economic, and cultural fields; call on Arab states to refrain from collaboration with Western companies seen to collaborate with SA; reemphasized the importance of the Arab oil boycott of SA and its commitment for its effective implementation; and denunciation of tanker companies helping SA to circumvent the oil embargo.

Nonaligned Countries

New Delhi (April 21, 1985): Support for mandatory sanctions against SA; call on member states of the nonaligned movement to sever all links and dealings with SA through the severance of diplomatic relations, observance of an oil embargo, disinvestment, prohibition of new investments, and the application of incentives to that end; prohibition of sale of Krugerrands and coins minted in SA; sports and cultural boycott; and withholding of overflight and landing facilities to aircraft, and docking rights to vessels.

_____Appendix C_____

Sanctions Bursting Strategies

_____Timothy U. Mozia_____

BRAZIL

Involvement in the explosives field through collaboration with the African Explosives and Chemical Industries of SA.

(*Source*: *Africa Confidential* 22, no. 3 [January 28, 1981], p. 8.)

BRUNEI

Was, until 1980, the only country that openly recorded crude oil exports to SA (869,000 tons in 1980). Though both Shell and BP ceased direct shipment to SA in 1980, there are speculations that other countries may well have continued.

(*Source*: *Africa Confidential* 24, no. 1 [January 5, 1983], p. 2.)

GERMANY, WEST

Direct Investment

Bank Loans. Between June 1982 and Dec. 1984, West German banks managed no less than 48 of the international loans in SA. This totalled 63% of all SA loans managed by international banks and 33% of all identified loans during this period. Prominent among these are the following:

- Dec. 1983 & Dec. 1984—The Deutsche Bank, Bayerische Vereinsbank, Commerzbank, Berliner Handels- und Frankfurter Bank, Bayerische Landesbank, Dresdner Bank, and Westdeutsche Landesbank-Girozentrale managed two separate loans of DM 200 million for SA.

- April 1985—SA Electricity Supply Commission (ESC) loan of DM 200 million was managed by Dresdner Bank accompanied by Commerzbank, Bayerische Hypotheken- und Wechselbank, Bayerische Vereinsbank, Berliner Handels- und Frankfurter Bank, Deutsche Bank, and Westdeutsche Landesbank- Girozentrale.

- June 1985—SA Transport Services (SATS) loan managed by a West German syndicate led by Deutsche Bank, BHF Bank, Commerzbank, Dresdner Bank, Bayerische Hypotheken- und Wechselbank, and Bayerische Vereinsbank. These also managed a DM 100 million loan issued by the SA Department of Post and Telecommunications in July 1985.

Arms

- Delivery of an estimated 300 "unimog" vehicles, ostensibly a multipurpose civilian vehicle, to SA. These vehicles are in fact used for military purposes in SA.

- Illegal shipments of military equipment by West Germany's major arms manufacturer, Rheinmetall, in 1980.

- Purchase of four BO 105 helicopters by the SA police from the Munich firm Messerschmitt-Bolkaw-Blohm (MBB).

- Development of a R 260 million plant for the production of standardized diesel engines used for military purposes by Daimler Benz via its SA subsidiary, United Car and Diesel Distributors, and Perkins Diesel, a subsidiary of Massey Ferguson.

The above instances of sanctions violation were confirmed by Mr. Abdul Minty, director of an Oslo-based institute that monitors adherence to the U.S. arms embargo on behalf of the United Nations.

(*Source*: *Transnational Corporations in South Africa and Namibia*, pp. 308–16.)

In addition, provision of components for the SA submarine, the Drakensberg, and sale of blueprints for the Construction of four submarines by the West German companies Howaldtswerke-Deutsche Werft (HDW), which is 75 percent government owned, and the Ingenieurkontor Lueck (IKL).

(*Source*: *Africa Confidential* 29, no. 6 [March 18, 1988], pp.1–2.)

IRAN

The purchase of arms and ammunition from SA. Between 1984 and 1985 no less than five cargoes, including detonators and shells for the G-5 long range artillery piece, went from SA to Iran. One cargo alone was valued at $29 million. SA supplied Iran with about 1,900 tons of arms during this period.

(*Source*: *Africa Confidential*, 28, no. 24 [December 2, 1987], p. 8.)

KENYA

Main refuelling point for aircrfaft heading for SA—17 of these flights touch down in Nairobi every week, including British Airways, Swissair, and Lufthansa.

(*Source*: *Africa Confidential*, 27, no. 17 [August 20, 1986], p. 6.)

NETHERLANDS

A major oil transhipment center used to "launder" supplies to SA. British North Sea oil that cannot be sold officially to SA is handled through Rotterdam. Most active in this Rotterdam-SA run is AP Moeller, the Danish company that since 1979 has sent in no less than eight tankers carrying 2 million tons of oil worth nearly $500 million.

(*Source*: *Africa Confidential*, 24, no. 1 [January 5, 1983], p. 2.)

OMAN

- Petroleum Development Oman sent at least six tankers of oil to SA between September 1979 and June 1980, carrying 1.4 million tons worth about $300 million.
- Transworld Oil, a Dutch-based trading company with heavy involvement in SA, was permitted to raise its lifting of Omani oil from 40,000 to 90,000 barrels a day in October 1981.

(*Source*: *Africa Confidential*, 24, no. 1 [January 5, 1983].)

POLAND

The purchase of Polish arms by Armscor subsidiaries. The companies involved are Exportex and the Iran International Trading Company. These bought ground-to-air and antitank missiles from Poland with the permission of the Polish Chamber of Commerce (CINZIN), 1980–1987.

(*Source*: *Africa Confidential*, 29, no. 12 [June 17, 1988].)

PORTUGAL

Arms. Transfer of six corvettes to the SA navy.

(*Source*: *African Confidential*, 20, no. 2 [October 17, 1979], p. 8.)

SAUDI ARABIA

- Alleged involvement in a $4.5 billion, three-year contact for 15 million tons of Saudi oil to SA through an intermediary, Marino Chiavelli—an Italian businessman.

- The supply of about 150,000 barrels per day of Saudi oil to SA through an Asian state acting as a front.

(*Source: Africa Confidential*, 24, no. 1 [January 5, 1983], pp. 1–2.)

SWAZILAND

Not only in virulent opposition to sanctions but also the most accommodationist toward repositioning of SA and foreign capital within its borders for the purpose of evading the intent of sanctions—amendment of tax laws in 1985 to favor investors using Swaziland as a reexporting base. In 1985, the Kirsch Group of SA established the SWATEX (now NATEX) textile manufacturing mill at Matsapha Industrial Park near Manzini; Taiwanese also set up four clothing factories; U.S.-based Coca-Cola repositioned itself at Matsapha with the construction of a $7.5 million concentrates plant in late 1986.

A partnership was established between the Commonwealth Development Corporation (CDC) and Swaziland's Tibiyo TakaNgwane—launching an ethanol fuels production plant in 1988 with potentials for energy supply to SA; the British industrial conglomerate Courtald's stake in the Usutu Pulp Company was purchased by SA's largest pulp and paper group, Sappi; and a ferrochrome plant was established by a consortium led by Australia Overseas Mining, Ltd., in 1988.

Swaziland's branch of an SA subsidiary (Camel Clothing) of Taiwan's Chia Ho business group is involved in exporting textiles made in SA to the United States routed through Swaziland. This practice is also confirmed in *Africa News*, Vol. 29, no. 12 (June 13, 1988) and the *Christian Science Monitor*, August 1988.

(*Source*: Booth, "South Africa's Hinterland.")

SWEDEN

- Loopholes in legislation—October 1987 Swedish Trade Boycott Act encourages sanctions bursting to the extent that it permits Swedish-owned subsidiary companies to continue trade with SA and Namibia. Those already with investments in SA may remain there.
- Saab—Scania trucks continue to roll on SA's export-import route.
- The sale of excavators and other earth-moving equipment to SA by VOLVO BM.
- ESAB, a Gothenburg welding company, does extensive business with SA.
- ASEA Electric SA—continued activity in SA through the SA company Powertech, to which it had sold its shares in January 1987. This company also continued business with SA through merger with the Swiss company Brown Boveri Company (BBC), with headquarters in Switzerland—a country known to have increased trade with SA when others sought the implementation of laws against it.

UNITED KINGDOM

Illegal Export of Embargoed Equipment to South Africa (SA).

- 1980—Supply of arms to SA by Leonard Hammond.
- October 18, 1982—Imprisonment of three British citizens at the Old Bailey for conspiring to smuggle arms worth one million pounds to SA.
- March 1984—Exposure of clandestine activities of SA Armscor agents in England, especially the case of the Coventry Four (Armscor operatives caught in numerous clandestine operations to obtain armaments).

Illegal Export of Dual-Purpose Equipment. Export of goods ostensibly for civilian rather than military use to SA. In some cases, items are reclassified as dual-purpose in order to permit their export to SA. These include civilian aircraft, radar with civil application, military communications, and computers.

British Company Subsidiaries in SA. Continued sabotage of the arms embargo by subsidiaries of British companies in SA that supply equipment to SA military police. These include:

- British Leyland—Supply of Landrovers and trucks.
- ICI—Supply of ammunition and explosives through its 40 percent holding in SA African Explosives and Chemical Industries (AECI).
- Trafalgar House—Supply of artillery shells through Cementation Engineering.
- ICL—Supply of computers to the SA military police.
- GEC—Supply of military communications equipment.
- Plessey—Supply of military communications equipment.
- BP and Shell—Oil and other petroleum products for the military and police. These undermine the embargo by: (1) manufacturing items in SA either under license or import of technology and know-how to parent company; (2) transfer of skilled personnel to SA on temporary or permanent assignment; and (3) provision of finance capital.

Licenses. Continued production of items of foreign origin by SA under license, e.g. the Rolls-Royce Viper engines used for production of the SA Impala 1 and 2 aircraft repeatedly involved in attacks against Angola.

Recruitment of Personnel. This includes direct recruitment of British military personnel and indirect recruitment of British citizens for helicopter development, munitions projects, high-technology manufactures, aircraft design, and numerous similar activities.

SA Visits, Exchanges, Diplomatic Representatives, etc. Free movement of persons of SA origin involved in arms deals in and out of Britain. For example,

Dirk Stoffer and known activities of SA diplomatic personnel in this regard in Britain. Little evidence of internal action by British government agencies to investigate such clandestine operations.

Spares, Maintenance, and Repair of Aircraft. Activities such as the continued maintenance of SA's 16 buccaneer aircraft supplied by Britain.

Nuclear Collaboration. Continued support of SA's nuclear buildup through recruitment of skilled and qualified personnel.

Military Collaboration. Direct military collaboration between Britain and SA was fully operational at least until late 1984, as, for example, in the exchange of naval intelligence between both countries.

(*Source: Transnational Corporations in South Africa and Namibia: United Nations Public Hearings,* Vol. 3, New York, 1987, pp. 255–308.)

USA

- Continued supply of electronics for military communication to SA, e.g. the TR 178, whose production was slated to commence in March 1985.
- Supply of computers for use by SA's arms makers—Armscor uses equipment from NCR, Burroughs, Hewlett-Packard, and Sperry to mention but a few.
- Outfitting the Council for Scientific and Industrial Research—Control Data Corporation, Amdahl, and IBM are the major suppliers for SA's Council for Scientific and Industrial Research (CSIR).
- High-tech sales to the SA government—Indispensable assistance from ITT in establishing a high-capacity telecommunications fiber optics link for SA's Postal Department.

(*Source: Transnational Corporations in South Africa and Namibia;* first and third items above also confirmed by George M. Houser, former executive secretary, American Committee on Africa, in "Relations between the United States and South Africa," submitted to the North American Regional Conference for Action against Apartheid, June 18–21, 1984.)

- Importation of uranium hexafluoride gas (uranium itself is banned) and certain steel alloys from SA by the US government.

(*Source;* Raymond W. Copson, specialist in international relations, Foreign Affairs and National Defense Division, in "South Africa: President's Report on Progress toward Ending Apartheid," CRS Report for Congress, October 19, 1987.)

Arms: An American aircraft firm, Globe Aero, Ltd., of Lakeland, Florida, supplied 21 aircraft to SA between March and May 1981. These planes are either delivered directly or through Belgium, France, Italy, and Gabon. These planes—

Piper, Beechcraft, and Mooney aircraft—are civilian aircraft but are ideal for aerial surveillance and reconnaissance missions.

(*Source: Africa Confidential*, 22, no. 19 [September 16, 1981], p. 8.)

Allegations of secret nuclear and military deals with SA and supply of military equipment to Bophutaswana, which has its own paramilitary police run by SA. In 1982, the air wing of the force bought two Helio Courier planes made by a division of General Aircraft Company of Bedford, Massachusetts, and an Italian-built surveillance aircraft powered by an AVCO Lycoming engine that is subject to U.S. export control.

(*Source: Africa Confidential*, 26, no. 5, [February 27, 1985], p. 8.)

Sports. The visit of the SA Springbok rugby team to the United States at the invitation of the Eastern Rugby Union of America, and the donation of 25,000 pounds sterling to that union by SA entrepreneur Louis Hoyt.

(*Source: Africa Confidential*, 22, no. 20 [September 30, 1981], p. 8.)

A general strategy is the sale of subsidiary companies to SA, but retaining rights to participate in vital decisions and share in profits, e.g. General Motors, International Business Machines (IBM), and Barclays Bank.

ZAMBIA

Initiation of direct flights to New York from Zambia with a predominantly white South African clientele.

(*Source*: Alan Booth, "South Africa's Hinterland: Swaziland's Role in Strategies for Sanctions Bursting," African Studies Association Paper, Chicago, October 1988.)

Sanctions against South Africa: A Bibliography

_____Timothy U. Mozia_____

Abernethy, D. B. "The Major Foreign Policy Positions of the Reagan Administration: Implications for United States–South-African Relations." _International Affairs Bulletin_ 5, no. 2 (1981): 18–44.

Akeroyd, Anne, et al. _European Business and South Africa: An Appraisal of the EC-Code of Conduct._ Munich: Kaiser, 1981.

Automating Apartheid: U.S. Computer Exports to South Africa and the Arms Embargo. Philadelphia, North American Research on the Military Industrial Complex (NARMIC)/American Friends Service Committee, 1982.

Aynor, H. S. "Israel versus Apartheid at the United Nations." _Jerusalem Journal of International Relations_ 8, no. 1 (March 1986): 34–41.

Baker, Pauline. "Facing Up to Apartheid." _Foreign Policy_ (Fall 1986): 37–62.

Baldwin, Brooke, and T. Brown. _Economic Action against Apartheid._ New York: Africa Fund, 1985.

Baldwin, David. _Economic Statecraft._ Princeton, N.J.: Princeton University Press, 1985.

Barber, James. "Economic Sanctions as a Policy Instrument." _International Affairs_ 55, no. 3 (July 1979): 385–401.

Barber, James, and M. Spicer. "Sanctions against South Africa: Option for the West." _International Affairs_ 55, no. 3 (July 1979): 385–401.

——— . "Sanctions and the Process of Adjustment." Mimeo. Johannesburg Consolidated Investments, Ltd., 1986.

Barber, James, et al. _The West and South Africa._ London: Routledge and Keagan Paul, 1982.

Becker, Charles M. "The Impact of Sanctions on South Africa and Its Periphery." *African Studies Review* 31, no. 2 (September 1988): 61–88.

Berridge, Geoff. "Apartheid and the West." *Year Book of World Affairs* 35 (1981): 152–164.

Bissel, R. E. *South Africa and the United States: The Erosion of an Influence Relationship*. New York: Praeger, 1982.

Bissel, R. E., and C. Crocker. *South Africa into the 1980s*. Boulder, Colo.: Westview Press, 1979.

Blumenfield, Jesmond. "Economic Sanctions against South Africa: Would They Work?" Mimeo. Brunel University, London, 1984.

————. "South Africa: Economic Responses to International Pressures." *World Today* 41, no. 12 (December 1985): 218–221.

Botha, P. W. "South Africa: Some Perspectives for the Future." *German Foreign Affairs Review* 35, no. 3 (1984): 272–280.

Brown-Leyton, David. *The Utility of International Economic Sanctions*. New York: St. Martin's Press, 1987.

Bunzel, J. H. "The Myth of the Laager: Using U.S. Business to Pressure South Africa." *Fletcher Forum* 5, no. 1 (1981): 133–139.

Campbell, Horace. "The Dismantling of the Apartheid War Machine." *Third World Quarterly* 9, no. 2 (April 1987): 468–492.

Carter, Barry E. *International Economic Sanctions: Improving the Haphazard U.S. Legal Regime*. New York: Cambridge University Press, 1988.

Carter, G. M. and P. O'Meara, eds. *Southern Africa: The Continuing Crisis*. Bloomington: Indiana University Press, 1979.

————. *International Politics in Southern Africa*. Bloomington: Indiana University Press, 1982.

Cawthra, Gavin. *Brutal Force: The Apartheid War Machine*. London: IDAF, 1986.

Chettle, John. "The United States and South Africa: Barriers to Communication." *Orbis* 25, no. 1 (Spring 1981): 145–163.

Clarke, Simon. *Changing Patterns of International Investment in South Africa and the Disinvestment Campaign*. London: Anti-Apartheid Movement, 1978.

Clough, Michael. "Beyond Constructive Engagement." *Foreign Policy* (Winter 1985/86): 3–24.

Coker, C. "South Africa's Strategic Importance: A Re-assessment." *Journal of the Royal United Services Institute for Defence Studies* 124, no. 4 (December 1979): 22–26.

————. "Collective Bargaining as an Internal Sanction: The Role of U.S. Corporations in South Africa." *Journal of Modern African Studies* 19, no. 4 (December 1981): 647–665.

————. "The United States and South Africa: Can Constructive Engagement Succeed?" *Millennium* 11, no. 3 (Autumn 1982): 223–241.

Congress of South Africa Trade Unions (COSATU). "Draft Report on the Effects of Sanctions." Mimeo, 1987.

Conrad, Thomas. "South Africa Circumvents Embargo." *Bulletin of the Atomic Scientists* 42, no. 3 (March 1986): 8–13.

Cooper, J. H. "Economic Sanctions and the South African Economy." *International Affairs Bulletin* 7, no. 2 (1983): 25–47.

──── . "Southern Africa and the Threat of Economic Sanctions." *African Journal of Economics* 52, no. 3 (1984). 266–281.

Crocker, Chester. *A U.S. Policy for the 80s*. Braamfontein, South Africa: South Africa Institute of International Affairs, 1981.

Cross, E. G. "Economic Sanctions as an Instrument of Policy: The Rhodesian Experience" *World Economy* (1981).

Danaher, Kevin. *South Africa and the United States: An Annotated Bibliography*. Washington, D.C.: Institute for Policy Studies, 1979.

──── . *In Whose Interest? A Guide to U.S.-South Africa Relations*. Washington, D.C.: Institute for Policy Studies, 1984.

──── . *The Political Economy of U.S. Policy Towards South Africa*. Boulder, Colo.: Westview Press, 1985.

Davenport, T. R. H. *South Africa: A Modern History*. London: Macmillan, 1985.

Davis, Jennifer, et al. "Economic Disengagement and South Africa: The Effectiveness and Feasibility of Implementing Sanctions and Divestment." *Law and Policy in International Business* 15, no. 2 (1983): 529–563.

Davis, S. C. *People's Sanctions Now*. New York: United Nations, 1987.

Declaration of the World Conference on Sanctions against South Africa. New York: United Nations, 1986.

Devereaux, J. A. *The Moral Dimensions of International Conduct*. Washington, D.C.: Georgetown University Press, 1983.

Doxey, M. *Economic Sanctions and International Enforcement*. New York: Oxford University Press, 1980.

──── . *International Sanctions in Contemporary Perspective*. New York: St. Martin's Press, 1987.

Eminent Persons Group (EPG). *Mission to South Africa: The Commonwealth Report*. Harmondsworth, England: Penguin, 1986.

Faltas, S. "Philips, Electronics and the Arms Trade." *Current Research on Peace and Violence* 4, no. 3 (1981): 195–217.

Federated Chambers of Industries. "The Effects of Sanctions on Employment and Production in South Africa." Mimeo, FCI, Pretoria, 1986.

Fisher, Scott. *Coping with Change: United States Policy Towards South Africa*. Washington, D.C.: National Defense University Press, 1982.

Fitzsimmons, P., and J. Bloch. *Arms for Apartheid: British Military Collaboration with South Africa*. London: Christian Concern for Southern Africa, 1981.

Franck, Thomas, et al. "An Investment Boycott by the Developing Countries against South Africa: A Rationale and Preliminary Assessment of Feasibility." *Human Rights Quarterly* 4, no. 3 (August 1982): 309–332.

Fraser, M. and O. Obasanjo. "What to Do about South Africa." *Foreign Affairs* 65, no. 1 (Fall 1986): 154–162.

Geldenhuys, Deon. "The United States and South Africa: A Dialogue of the Deaf?" *International Affairs Bulletin* 4, no. 1 (1980): 21–27.

──── . *The Diplomacy of Isolation: South African Foreign Policy Making*. New York: St. Martin's Press, 1984.

———, ed. *Sanctions against South Africa*. Johannesburg: South African Institute for International Affairs, 1979.

Gosiger, Mary. "Strategies for Divestment from United States Companies and Financial Institutions Doing Business with or in South Africa." *Human Rights Quarterly* 8, no. 3 (August 1986): 517–539.

Green, Reginald. *The Impact of Sanctions on South African Economics*. London: Stanhope Press, 1981.

———. "The SADCC Economies and Sanctions against South Africa." Mimeo. Institute of Development Studies, Sussex, 1986.

Hanlon, Joseph. *Apartheid's Second Front*. Harmondsworth, England: Penguin, 1986.

———. *Beggar Your Neighbors*. Bloomington: Indiana University Press, 1986.

Hanlon, Joseph and Roger Omond. *The Sanctions Handbook*. Harmondsworth, England: Penguin, 1987.

Harris, L. "South Africa's External Debt Crisis." *Third World Quarterly* (July 1986).

Hauck, David, et al. *Two Decades of Debate: The Controversy over U.S. Companies in South Africa*. Washington, D.C.: Investor Responsibility Research Center, 1983.

Hayes, J. P. *Economic Effects of Sanctions on Southern Africa*. London: Trade Policy Research Center, 1987.

Hermele, Kenneth, and Bertil Oden. "Sanctions Dilemmas: Some Implications of Economic Sanctions against South Africa." Discussion Paper No. 1, Uppsala, Sweden: Scandinavian Institute of African Studies, 1988.

Hufbauer, G., and J. Schott. *Economic Sanctions in Support of Foreign Policy Goals*. Washington, D.C.: Institute for International Economics, 1983.

———. *Economic Sanctions Reconsidered: History and Current Policy*. Washington, D.C.: Institute for International Economics, 1985.

Husain, Azim. "The West, South Africa and Israel: A Strategic Triangle." *Third World Quarterly* 4, no. 1 (January 1982): 44–73.

International Sanctions. Report by Group of the Royal Institute of International Affairs, London, 1938.

Kaempfer, W. and A. Lowenberg. "A Model of the Political Economy of International Investment Sanctions: The Case of South Africa." *Kyklos* 39, no. 3 (1986): 377–396.

Kanton, B., and D. Rees. *South African Economic Issues*. Capetown: Juta & Co., 1982.

Karis, Thomas. "Revolutions in the Making: Black Politics in South Africa." *Foreign Affairs* 62, no. 2 (Winter 1983/84): 378–406.

Keller, E. J., and L. A. Picard, eds. *South Africa in Southern Africa: Domestic Change and Internal Conflict*. Boulder, Colo.: Lynne Rienner, 1989.

Khalifa, Ahmed M. "Assistance to Racist Regimes in Southern Africa: Impact on the Enjoyment of Human Rights." Geneva: United Nations, 1979.

Khan, H. A. "Measuring and Analyzing the Economic Effects of Trade Sanctions against South Africa." *Africa Today*. vols. 2 & 3 (1986): 47–58.

———. *The Political Economy of Sanctions against Apartheid*. Boulder, Colo.: Lynne Rienner, 1989.

Klare, Michael T. "Evading the Embargo: Illicit U.S. Arms Transfers to South Africa." *Journal of International Affairs* 35, no. 1 (Spring/Summer 1981): 15–28.

Knorr, Klaus, and F. Trager, eds. *Economic Issues and National Security.* Regents Press of Kansas, 1977.

Landgren, Signe. "South Africa: Arms Embargo Disimplemented." *Bulletin of Peace Proposals* 17, nos. 3/4 (1986): 455–459.

Leape, Jonathan, et al., eds. *Business in the Shadow of Apartheid: U.S. Firms in South Africa.* Lexington, Mass.: Lexington Books, 1985.

Leggassick, Martin. "South Africa: Capital Accumulation and Violence." *Economy and Society* 3, no. 3 (1974): 253–291.

Legum, Colin. *South Africa: Crisis for the West.* New York: Praeger, 1964.

———. *The Western Crisis over Southern Africa: South Africa, Rhodesia, Namibia.* New York: Africana Publ. Co., 1979.

Leonard, Richard. *South Africa at War: White Power and the Crisis in South Africa.* Westport, Conn.: Lawrence Hill, 1983.

———. "The Crisis in South Africa: Rising Pressures on Multinationals." *Multinational Business* no. 3 (1986): 17–29.

Lewis, Neil. "West Finds Some Common Ground on Sanctions." *New York Times.* August 6, 1986.

Lipton, M. *Capitalism & Apartheid: South Africa 1910–1984.* Totowa, N.J.: Rowman & Allenheld, 1985.

———. *Sanctions and South Africa: The Dynamics of Economic Isolation.* London: Economic Intelligence Unit, 1988.

Lodge, T. *Black Politics in South Africa since 1945.* Johannesburg: Ravan Press, 1983.

Losman, Donald. *International Economic Sanctions.* Albuquerque: University of New Mexico Press, 1980.

Love, Janice. *The U.S. Anti-Apartheid Movement.* New York: Praeger, 1985.

Lundahl, M. "Economic Effects of a Trade and Investment Boycott against South Africa." *Scandinavian Journal of Economics* 86, no. 1 (1984): 68–83.

Maddrey, W. T. "Economic Sanctions against South Africa: Problems and Prospects for Enforcement of Human Rights Norms." *Virginia Journal of International Law* 22, no. 2 (Winter 1982): 345–380.

Magyar, Karl P. "The American Disinvestment in South Africa Debate: Short-Term Morality vs. Long-Term Economic Development." *International Affairs Bulletin* 9, no 1 (1985): 28–48.

Maull, H. W. "South Africa's Minerals: The Achilles Heel of Western Economic Security?" *International Affairs* 62, no. 4 (Autumn 1986): 619–626.

Mayall, J. "The Sanctions Problem in International Economic Relations." *International Affairs* 60, no. 4 (Autumn 1984): 631–643.

McGrath, M. D., and C. Jenkins. "The Economic Implications of Disinvestment for the South African Economy." Mimeo. Natal University, Durban, 1985.

McVeigh, Patrick. *Out of South Africa: The Insight Study of the South African Divestment Movement.* Boston: Insight, July 1986.

Memelstein, David. *The Anti-Apartheid Reader.* New York: Grove, 1987.

Minter, William. "South Africa: Straight Talk on Sanctions." *Foreign Policy* no. 65 (Winter 1986/87): 43–63.

Moorsom, R. *The Scope for Sanctions*. London: Catholic Institute for International Relations, 1986.

Myers, Desaix, et al. *U.S. Business in South Africa: The Economic, Political, and Moral Issues*. Bloomington: Indiana University Press, 1980.

Nicol, Davidson. "United States Foreign Policy in Southern Africa: Third World Perspectives." *Journal of Modern African Studies* 21, no. 4 (December 1983): 587–603.

Nolutshungu, Sam C. "Skeptical Notes on Constructive Engagement." *Issue* 12, nos. 3/4 (Fall/Winter 1982): 3–7.

Olivier, G. C. "South Africa's Response to Shifting Nuances in United States Foreign Policy." *Africa Insight* 12, no. 2 (1982): 85–88.

Omond, Roger. *The Apartheid Handbook*. Harmondsworth, England: Penguin, 1986.

Orkin, Mark. *Disinvestment: The Struggle and the Future*. Johannesburg: Ravan Press, 1986.

———. *The Struggle and the Future: What Black South Africans Really Think*. Johannesburg: Ravan Press. 1986.

Osborn, E. *South Africa under Sanctions*. Johannesburg: Ivor Jones, 1986.

Ozgur, O. A. *Apartheid: The United Nations and Peaceful Change in South Africa*. New York: Transnational Publishers. 1982.

Padayachee, Vishnu. "The Politics of International Economic Relations: South Africa and the International Monetary Fund. 1975 and Beyond." Paper presented to the Conference on the South African Economy after Apartheid. Center for Southern African Studies. York: University of York, September 1986.

Patel, C. N. "The Politics of State Expulsion from the United Nations: South Africa a Case in Point." *Comparative and International Law Journal of Southern Africa* 13, no. 3 (November 1980): 310–323.

Porter, R. "International Trade and Investment Sanctions: Potential Impact on the South African Economy." *Journal of Conflict Resolution* 23, no. 4 (December 1979): 579–612.

Price, M. R. and C. G. Rosberg. *The Apartheid Regime*. Berkeley: Regents, 1980.

Relly, Gavin. "The Costs of Disinvestment." *Foreign Policy* no. 63 (Summer 1986): 131–146.

"Republic of South African Foreign Trade Statistics." Pretoria, 1985.

Rich, Paul. "Insurgency, Terrorism and the Apartheid System in South Africa." *Political Studies* 32, no. 1 (March 1984): 68–85.

Rogers, Barbara, and Brian Bolton. *Sanctions against South Africa: Exploding the Myths*. London: Manchester Free Press, 1981.

St. John, Jorre de. *A House Divided: South Africa Faces Uncertain Future*. New York: Carnegie Endowment for International Peace, 1977.

Scarritt, James R. "The External Pressures on Human Rights in South Africa: Problems of Research and Design." Paper presented at the Annual Meeting of the African Studies Association, Baltimore, 1978.

Schmidt, Elizabeth. *Decoding Corporate Camouflage: U.S. Business Support for Apartheid*. Washington, D.C.: Institute for Policy Studies, 1980.

————. *One Step in the Wrong Direction: An Analysis of the Sullivan Principles.* New York: Episcopal Churchpeople for a Free Southern Africa, 1985.

————. *United Nations Sanctions and South Africa: Lessons from the Case of Southern Rhodesia.* New York: United Nations, 1987.

Schoeman, Elna, ed. *South Africa and the United Nations: A Select and Annotated Bibliography.* Braamfontein, South Africa: South Africa Institute of International Affairs, 1981.

Segal, Ronald, ed. *Sanctions against South Africa.* Baltimore, Penguin, 1964.

Shepherd, George W., Jr. *Anti-Apartheid: Transnational Conflict and Western Policy in the Liberation of South Africa.* Westport, Conn.: Greenwood Press, 1977.

————. *The Trampled Grass: Tributary States and Self-Reliance in the Indian Ocean Zone of Peace.* Westport, Conn.: Greenwood Press, 1987.

Spandau, A. *Economic Boycott against South Africa: Normative and Factual Issues.* Cape Town: Juta, 1979.

Spicer, Michael. *Sanctions against South Africa: The Changing Context.* Braamfontein, South Africa: South African Institute of International Affairs, 1982.

Study Commission on U.S. Policy toward Southern Africa. *South Africa: Time Running Out.* Berkeley: University of California Press, 1981.

Sullivan, Leon. *The Role of Multinational Corporations in South Africa.* Johannesburg: South African Institute of Race Relations, 1980.

————. "Agents for Change: The Mobilization of Multinational Companies in South Africa." *Law and Policy in International Business* 15, no 2 (1983): 427–444.

Sunter, C. *The World and South Africa in the 1990s.* Cape Town: Human and Rosseau, 1987.

Svetic, F. "Sanctions: What Kind and against Whom?" The Power and Impotence of the International Penalty Mechanism." *Review of International Affairs* (December 1986): 22–24.

Ungar, Sanford, and P. Vale. "South Africa: Why Constructive Engagement Failed." *Foreign Affairs* 64, no. 2 (Winter 1985/86): 234–258

Unified List of United States Companies with Investments or Loans in South Africa and Namibia. New York: The Africa Fund, 1985.

United Nations. *Sanctions against South Africa: The Peaceful Alternative to Violent Change.* New York: United Nations, 1988.

United Nations. *Transnational Corporations in South Africa and Namibia: United Nations Public Hearings,* vol. 2. New York: United Nations, 1986.

United Nations. *Transnational Corporations in South Africa and Namibia: United Nations Public Hearings,* vol. 3. New York: United Nations, 1987.

United Nations General Assembly. *Resolutions Adopted by the United Nations General Assembly on the Question of Apartheid (1962–1986).* New York: United Nations, April 1987.

United Nations General Assembly. *Resolutions on Apartheid Adopted by the United Nations General Assembly in 1987.* New York: United Nations, December 1987.

U.S. Congress. House Committee on Foreign Affairs. Subcommittee on Africa. *Economic Sanctions and Their Potential Impact on U.S. Corporate*

Involvement in South Africa. Hearing before the Subcommittee on Africa of the Committee on Foreign Affairs. Washington, D.C.: GPO, January 31, 1985.

U.S. Department of State. *United States and South Africa: US Public Statements and Related Documents 1977–1985.* Washington, D.C.: Office of the Historian, Department of State, 1985.

————. *Report of the Secretary of State's Advisory Committee on South Africa.* Washington, D.C.: GPO, 1987.

Wallensteen, P., and M. Nincic, eds. *Dilemmas of Economic Coercion.* New York: Praeger, 1983.

Wolf, Charles. *International Economic Sanctions.* Santa Monica, Calif.: Rand Corp., 1980.

Wolpe, Harold. "Capitalism and Cheap Labor Power in South Africa: From Segregation to Apartheid." *Economy and Society* 1, no. 4 (1972): 425–456.

Wright, Sanford. "Comprehensive International Sanctions against South Africa." *Africa Today* 33, nos. 2–3 (1986): 5–24.

Index

Index

About the Contributors

STEPHEN P. DAVIS is Senior Analyst at the Investor Responsibility Research Center, Washington, D.C., and author of *Apartheid Rebels*.

HAIDER ALI KHAN is Associate Professor of International and Development Economics at the Graduate School of International Studies, University of Denver. He recently published *The Political Economy of Sanctions against Apartheid*.

TIMOTHY U. MOZIA is from Nigeria and a Ph.D. candidate at the Graduate School of International Studies, University of Denver.

VED P. NANDA is Professor and Director of the International Legal Studies Program at the College of Law, University of Denver. He is an international lawyer and has published in the fields of international law and human rights. He recently co-edited and contributed to *Refugee Law and Policy* (Greenwood Press, 1989).

GEORGE W. SHEPHERD, JR., is Professor of International Relations and Director of the Consortium on Human Rights Development at the Graduate School of International Studies, University of Denver. He has published widely in the fields of African studies and human rights. Among his works are *Emerging Human Rights* (Greenwood

Press, forthcoming) and *The Trampled Grass: Tributary States and Self-Reliance in the Indian Ocean Zone of Peace* (Praeger, 1987).

SANFORD WRIGHT is Professor of Political Science at the California State University at Chico. He specializes in southern Africa studies. Among his publications is "Comprehensive International Sanctions against South Africa," which appeared in *Africa Today* in 1986.